CONFESSIONS OF
BOYHOOD

JOHN ALBEE

Confessions of Boyhood

John Albee

© 1st World Library, 2006
PO Box 2211
Fairfield, IA 52556
www.1stworldlibrary.com
First Edition

LCCN: 2006936204

Softcover ISBN: 978-1-4218-3067-4
Hardcover ISBN: 978-1-4218-2967-8
eBook ISBN: 978-1-4218-3167-1

Purchase *"Confessions of Boyhood"*
as a traditional bound book at:
www.1stWorldLibrary.com/purchase.asp?ISBN=978-1-4218-3067-4

1st World Library is a literary, educational organization dedicated to:

- Creating a free internet library of downloadable ebooks

- Hosting writing competitions and offering book publishing scholarships.

Interested in more 1st World Library books?
contact: literacy@1stworldlibrary.com
Check us out at: www.1stworldlibrary.com

1ˢᵗ World Library Literary Society

Giving Back to the World

"If you want to work on the core problem, it's early school literacy."
- James Barksdale, former CEO of Netscape

"No skill is more crucial to the future of a child, or to a democratic and prosperous society, than literacy."
- Los Angeles Times

Literacy... means far more than learning how to read and write... The aim is to transmit... knowledge and promote social participation."
- UNESCO

"Literacy is not a luxury, it is a right and a responsibility. If our world is to meet the challenges of the twenty-first century we must harness the energy and creativity of all our citizens."
- President Bill Clinton

"Parents should be encouraged to read to their children, and teachers should be equipped with all available techniques for teaching literacy, so the varying needs and capacities of individual kids can be taken into account."
- Hugh Mackay

CONTENTS

INTRODUCTION 7
THE WALLS OF THE WORLD 19
SHADOWS AND ECHOES 32
HOLIDAYS... 37
THE AMPUTATION.. 39
COUNTRY FUNERALS 47
MY MOTHER'S RED CLOAK.................................. 52
MY UNCLE LYMAN 57
THE ANCIENT NEW ENGLAND FARMER.......... 71
THE DORR WAR AND MILLERISM 73
WOODS AND PASTURES 77
APPRENTICESHIPS 86
    HOME AND HOMESICKNESS........................ 86
    THE SAW MILL... 91
    BOOTMAKING.. 99
    LOVE AND LUXURY 103
    SHOP BOY 112
    PISTOL MAKER 119
    THE AWAKENING 124
    STUDENT LIFE..134
    SCHOOL MASTER 140
    FARM HAND..148
CONCLUSION..154
AVE ATGUE VALE..156

INTRODUCTION

For so many years Bellingham has had its abode in my fancy that I find it hard to associate the town with a definite geographical location. I connect it rather with the places of dreams and wonderland; the lost cities of the Oxus and Hydaspes, the Hesperian Gardens and those visionary realms visited and named by poets. My birthplace grows unfamiliar when I take down an atlas and run my finger over the particolored divisions of the Norfolk County of Massachusetts and trace the perimeter which confines Bellingham to its oblong precinct, surrounded by those mythical lands of Mendon, Milford and Medway. They wear an authoritative appearance on the map; but for me they occupied no such positions in my childhood and stand as stubborn realities hindering my feet when I wish to return to the Red House of my fathers. Once there, memory and fact are no longer conflicting. I find, as of old, the gently undulating hills, the gently loitering stream.

The legends concerning the founding of Bellingham are missing. I am sorry; for I could believe the most extravagant, feeling with Plutarch, that fortune, in the history of any town, often shows herself a poet. The Delphian Pythoness advised Theseus to found a city wherever in a strange land he was most sorrowful and afflicted. There at length he would find repose and happiness. Thus it happened when the wanderers from Braintree settled on the shores of the upper Charles. They brought their unhappy fortunes so far, and there, in due time, found comfort and contentment.

The traveller, journeying through the highways of Bellingham, would see nothing to attract his attention or interest. It has no monuments, ruins nor historic associations; no mountain, nor hill even. The Charles river has travelled so little way from its source as hardly yet to be a river. The soil is stony and pays back not much more than is put into it. The fine forests of white oak have been mostly reduced to ashes in the stoves of Milford, and their oracles have ceased. My father, who could cut as clean a scarf as any man of his day, helped to fell them. Scrub oak and gray birch have taken their places, but do not fill them. One great elm remains; it seemed to me the largest and oldest tree in the world. My mother nursed her children in its shade; under it my world began. In its top lived the wind and from the longest spray of its longest limb the oriole hung her artistic basket and brooded her golden babies. Like many another ancient dooryard tree it carried back its traditional origin to a staff stuck in the ground and left to its fate.

Bellingham was incorporated in 1719 by yeoman farmers, and later settled largely by Revolutionary soldiers from neighboring communities on the east, particularly from old Braintree. On the Mendon tablet placed in memory of the founders of the town appears the name of my earliest ancestor. He was a surveyor and plotted the land and built the first mill, being called from Braintree for that purpose. Permit me to take pride in my learned ancestor, especially in his talent for figures—the distress of my life. The most interesting periods in the annals of the New England people are when they began to organize themselves into communities for the promotion of law, learning and piety. Their efforts were primitive yet affecting. Their language halted, but they knew what they wanted and meant to have.

Such are the records of Bellingham. And other history it has little out of the common incidents of humanity. No eminent sons have as yet remembered it with noble benefactions. It has had no poet and no mention in literature. The reporters pass it by. It is not even a suburb, last sad fate of many towns and villages. This is one of the reasons for my attachment—its unchangeableness, its entire satisfaction of sentiment.

Yet such is the charm of one's native soil that he is able to find in it the most wonderful of all the beautiful things of the soul, namely, those which no one else can see or believe. After long years of absence, on returning to Bellingham, my memory sees more than my eyes. She who accompanies me in my rambles over the town often takes photographs of the places dearest to me; but her pictures show not what I behold, and she wonders what it can be that so infatuates me. I see a hand she cannot see—forms, faces, happenings not registered on the camera; places where linger the invisible spirits of joyful or painful experiences; playmates, companions, whole families now dust, a thousand events recalled only when time begins to obliterate those of the present moment.

Although the sun went down over venerable Mendon town, it lingered longer over Bellingham in summer days than in any place I have known. There was hardly any night; just a few attic stairs, a dream, and the sun and I were again at play. Nor elsewhere were ever the summer clouds so high, so near the blue, so impetuous in the constant west wind to follow each other into the unknown, mysterious east.

Fortunate is the town with a river flowing through its whole length and boys and girls to accompany its unhasting waters. It was made for them, also for the little fish and the white scented lilies. For a few hours of the day the great floats of the mill wheel drank of it, sending it onward in the only agitation it ever permitted itself. Then there was Bear Hill, though never a bear in the oldest memory, yet the name was ominous to children. I feared it and liked to visualize its terrors from a safe distance in the blackberry field behind the Red House. To kill a bear or an Indian was the very limit of imaginative prowess. It was too easy, and in an hour, tiresome, to kill birds, snakes and anything one chanced upon that had life. Only the grasshopper could escape with the ransom of some molasses from the jug he carries hidden, no one knows where. You never knew a grasshopper was provisioned with a molasses jug?

Well then you have never studied the boy's traditional natural history. Therein are recorded things unknown to science; discoveries never divulged, secrets more deep than the Elusinian, passed on from initiate to initiate for countless generations. Nature has told them only to children, and when grown to manhood, seals their lips with that impious injunction to put away childish things.

It is not a river nor a landscape that gives to a town its real importance; it is the character of its men and women. That is the pinnacle from which to view its landscape. Before cities and factories had begun to stir the ambition and attract the young by opportunities for fortune and fame, Bellingham was the home of an intelligent, liberty-loving people; a community self-sufficing, sharing its abundance with those less abounding. It was thus the best place in the world to be born about the first third of the last century—to be explicit, in eighteen hundred and thirty-three. And I wish that I and the companions of my childhood could have imitated Plutarch who said "I live in a little town and choose to live there lest it should become smaller."

All that is dear remains as it was, and it is my delight to remember and magnify what it is to me. My friends laugh when I say it is better to be remembered in Bellingham than to be famous in ten cities. It has been my misfortune never to have lived in any other place that in a few years, did not change and forget itself. I cannot find anything in my later residences that continues to connect me with them. They have cut a street through me, they have torn down and rebuilt my old nests; and I know no more melancholy intimation of the small consequence of one's life and associations than this. Therefore I thank Heaven for a town removed from the track of progress, uninvaded by summer visitors and all business enterprises; land left sacred to its native inhabitants, a sluggish stream, unprofitable earth, huckleberry bushes and the imagination. Since this is so, and there is little fear of intrusion by the curious or the mercenary, I will confide to my readers the situation of the town with the understanding that they will never attempt to verify my description.

It lies in the southwestern corner of Norfolk county, is eight miles long from north to south, from three to four in width. The brooks and ponds in the southern part have their outlet into the Blackstone river; those of the north into the Charles, which is the natural but tortuous bound between eighteen towns and cities of the county. It was named for one of the Provincial governors of Massachusetts, Richard Bellingham—a fine name. Farming is the chief occupation of the inhabitants at present as it always has been. In former times there were two or three small cotton and woollen mills on the river. The oldest of them, on the banks of the Charles, is as picturesque a ruin as time, fire and neglect are able to achieve in a hundred years. The walls of heavy blocks of stone, roofless and broken in outline, are still standing. Great trees have grown up within them and now overtop them. Here and there a poplar leans forth from a broken window casement, leaving scant room for the ghosts of ancient spinners and weavers to peer into the outer world at midnight. From a distance it resembles a green, enclosed orchard. Decay may mantle itself in newest green but cannot obliterate memories of former generations. On these fallen floors the young women of Bellingham once labored and were merry on fifty cents a day, a working day never less than twelve hours long. They sang at their work, and when the loom was running in good order, they leaned out of the windows or gossiped with each other. On Sundays the roads and fields were gay with these respectable Yankee maidens, becurled and beribboned, philandering with their sweethearts or in bevies visiting each other's houses. Every girl had her album in which her friends wrote their names, and usually they were able to contribute an original stanza; or, if not, a line from the hymn-book, or a sentiment from the school reader or Bible. They dressed in calico in summer and in winter linsey-woolsey, and wore at their work ample aprons of osnaburg, a small checked blue and white cloth. Vice was unknown; at least the annals record no flagrant examples.

I fear those who only know the cotton and woollen mills of

this day cannot realize or believe what an immense blessing they were to New England when they first began to dot all the streams offering sufficient water power to operate their machinery. For the first time they opened a way for young women to earn money whereby they could assist their families and promote the improvement of their own condition. Work in these mills was sought as a temporary employment generally; or for the purpose of gaining money enough to attend an academy for a few terms, from whence they were graduated qualified to teach a district school. It is said, that formerly, when the factory girls were all American, five hundred could have been found at any time in the Lowell mills competent to teach school. What a contrast these girls were in health, beauty and intelligence to the pale, pinched faces and bedraggled dresses now seen hurrying to the Fall River and Manchester mills. The mill girls of 1840 were self-respecting, neat in their dress, religious, readers of good books, members of all kinds of clubs for study, and many of them could write excellent English. The *Lowell Offering*, a magazine conducted by factory girls at the period I have mentioned, now seems very remarkable; not so much perhaps for its contributions, as that it should have existed at all. Yet the writing in the *Operatives' Magazine* and the *Lowell Offering* was as good as that now appearing in periodicals, in some respects superior, being the free, unpaid and spontaneous utterances of the human heart. It is mentioned with praise in Emerson's *Dial*. One of our sweetest New England poets, Lucy Larcom, began her career as a writer in them. I write that name where I can see from my window a mountain named in her honor. Although her childhood was widely different from mine in outward circumstances, I find in her autobiography something of her inward experiences that reminds me of my own.

All the old-time life of farm and factory is gone. It is refreshing to know a single remnant of it left anywhere; and I was never more surprised and delighted than to find in Florence, Massachusetts, a few years ago, a large class of silk mill girls reading and studying Chaucer under the direction of a farmer's wife of the same place. Bellingham mill, may you continue to be filled with goodly trees until you can assemble a class in Chaucer!

Near this ruined mill stands a row of tenement houses fast falling to pieces and one large house where some of the operatives were boarded. In the neighboring hamlet nearly every house is standing that was there fifty years ago, and there are no new ones. There was an ancient law of Solon that houses in the country should be placed a bowshot apart, and this regulation seems to have been observed in Bellingham. You could see their lights in the evening, hear the dogs bark and the cock crow at dawn.

Over the Green Store is a hall where formerly Adin Ballou used to preach his various gospels of Universalism, temperance, peace and abolition on Sunday afternoons following the morning services in his neighboring parish, the Hopedale Community. As my family was attached to the Baptist and Methodist persuasions I cannot now imagine what drew them to hear this famous reformer of society and religion. They must have attended in this hall, for although I cannot recall anything else, I do remember going to sleep there in the hot summer afternoons in my sister's lap. But any kind of a meeting was a temptation not to be resisted in that little community. Adin Ballou was in full sympathy with all the other reformers and transcendentalists of the Commonwealth, and when I search myself for an explanation of my early and intuitive attraction to their ideals I sometimes fancy they must have visited me in my sleep in that old hall; or perhaps I heard something which lay like a seed in the unconscious, secret recesses of my being until time and favoring circumstances called it forth. For I find it recorded, that he fired his hearers with aspirations for "grand objects and noble ideas."

Regarding the topography of Bellingham, the most that can be said is, that it has none, none that distinguishes it either by lakes or hills. The best soil is in the northern and southern parts of the town and along the valley of the Charles river. The white oaks were once the most abundant of the deciduous trees. They seem to love a lean and stubborn soil. I have seen graves laid open to a considerable depth where oaks had once stood, and still uncovering nothing but coarse gravel. I have talked with ancient well-diggers who declared that the bottom of Bellingham was just like the top and only good for grey birch and beans. Yet they may not have dug after all to the veins which supply the floral and arboreal life of the earth. A poor soil is usually porous, admitting more wholesome air and sunshine, and it is through these vital forces that trees and men grow taller and hardier. Thus do I like to compensate the sterile fields of my native place by their stalwart, thin, straight-backed citizens, all bone and muscle, living with undimmed eyes and ears to ripe old age, mowing their meadows to the last summer of their lives and dying conveniently in some winter month when work was slack.

The dial of my childhood marked none but sunny days; the dry air and drier earth of Bellingham gave me health and strength. I never found any road in the town too long for my walking if only the summer afternoon were as long. I knew the roads and byways foot by foot, and could find my way, if need were, in the night as well as in the day. All the houses I knew and their occupants; all the good apple trees and whose was every cow grazing in the roadside pastures or resting beneath a tree. If I could have my will I would spend the remainder of my days rambling once more and every day those familiar roads and lanes, like Juno descending the Olympian path—

> "Reflecting with rapid thoughts
> There was I, and there, remembering many things."

The most perfect picture of contentment is a cow lying in the green grass under a green tree chewing her cud; and this contentment I could realize, give me back the sandy highways and green meadows, my bare feet, idleness and long summer days.

I was even more familiar with the pastures and the woods than with the roads. The whole surface of my ambit was spread out like a miniature map in my eye, and continues to be. Especially I knew the convenient ways of reaching the river and Beaver pond and the brook which connects it with the river Charles. It grieves me that this stream has never been celebrated in verse or prose; while the Concord, which rises on the same watershed with the Charles and almost from the same spring, has had several famous poets and is historic in Revolutionary annals. Longfellow sang one short song to our river, but he looked out only on the foul mudbanks of its Cambridge course, shut the door, went back to his study and composed his subjective Charles.

Slowly did I learn the actual extent and course of the river Charles which, in my childhood, rose as a shallow stream in the green depths of a wood lying to the north of Bellingham, flowing east, then south under the arched bridge near the school house, emptying somewhere in the southern sky; for, in my childish apprehension, I thought it must run up from where I was most familiar with it. Its youth and mine were coincident, and as years were added, the river broadened and lengthened until I found myself one day at its mouth, in reaching which, it had touched and watered eighteen towns. It is the father of no considerable stream, but innumerable rivulets add to its waters. It is about thirty miles from source to mouth in a direct course though it wanders a hundred miles in its efforts to find the ocean.

> "There runs a shallow brook across our field
> For twenty miles where the black crow flies five."

It never has any headlong haste to arrive. It saunters like a schoolboy and stops to visit a thousand recesses and indentations of upland and meadow. It stays for a cow to drink, or an alder to root itself in the bank, or to explore a swamp, and it rather wriggles than runs through its eighteen townships. It is likely to stop at any one of them and give up the effort to reach the sea. For my part I wish it had, and actually, as in my memory and fancy, ended at the outermost shores of Bellingham.

The revolution of the earth can only account for the flow of the Charles for there is no perceptible descent of the land. I like to think it is ruled by the stars and not by the configuration of the earth's surface. It is vagrant and nomadic in its habits, moving on a little, returning, winding and doubling, uncertain of its own intentions, a brother of the English Wye, said to derive its name from *Vaga*, the wanderer, or vagabond. Since its waters sprang from their fountain head and learned that their destiny was to become a river, they have never been in haste to reach its turbid outlet, but go reluctantly from town to town with whole days before them, yes, perhaps, it was an age in making its first journey. It loses its way often, but cares not so there be a pleasant meadow to meander through or a contemplative fisherman to companion its course. The Charles has never gained force, as man is said to do, by having obstacles to overcome. It treats all the dams which intercept its current with a lenient benevolence, never having been known to carry one away. Meeting a dam, it turns the other cheek; in other words it patiently retires into its higher channels and fountains, filling and stilling the little babbling brooks by its backward impulse, contented to be a pond when it cannot be a river. It scarcely resisted the ancients of Dedham, when they attempted to steal it. Having no watershed of its own, the Charles is not subject to those floods and frenzies which make so many other streams dangerous. Sedges and flags, the skunk cabbage and marsh marigold, grape vines, alders, willows and button bush abound along its shores. White and yellow lilies and the pickerel weed almost choke its course in many places. Under the leaves of these hides himself that fish which old anglers named the water-wolf, the pickerel, who preys upon his smaller brothers and sisters. All is fish that comes into his net. There was no more exciting moment in my boyhood than when a pickerel swallowed the frog's leg on my hook and began to retreat with it under the lily pads. In the stream also were horned pouts, perch, shiners and that silly little fish we called "kivers," for which my earliest fishing was done with a bent pin. I was naturally capacitated for fishing by my fondness for silence and solitude. The mystery of water drew me from one pool to another and a constant expectancy of a larger fish than had ever been caught. I was not aware that words could make him as big as one chose; but I had pictured him in my mind in all his immense and shining length. What I most wished to catch was a leviathan; my mother when reading the word in the Bible had told me it meant some kind of great fish, the largest in the world. Once indeed I thought I had him on my hook, but it proved only a sunken log. Of stillness and solitude I had my fill strolling along the banks of the river. It seemed like Sunday without the requirements imposed upon me by that day, stiff shoes and Sunday-school. I became as still as the nature around me, stepping softly and almost hushing my breath. If I might describe in one word the sensation which I commonly experienced in my earliest lonely intercourse with stream and forest it was a breathless expectation, made up in part of fear, in part of a vague hope of discovering something wonderful. This quest never wearied nor disheartened me; I only became more eager in its pursuit the more it evaded me; another search, another day and it would be revealed. What would be revealed? There are no words given to man in which he can clearly portray the striving of the spirit for that which shall resemble and satisfy its visions and aspirations. The child sees these visions and feels these aspirations and strives to put his finger upon them; they exist for him as physical objects which he wishes to capture and carry home to his mother with a proud consciousness of his valor. As soon as she had praised my handful of flowers, my pocketful of nuts, or little string of fish they palled upon me and I began immediately to feel an uneasy sense of disappointment, of disillusion, knowing I had miserably failed. The bombastic brag to my mother and her praise were a kind of mockery and falsehood. Illusion followed illusion, defeat followed defeat, yet the morrow was ever to be their healer and compensation. How often have I been soothed by the waveless waters of the Charles river, its whispering ripples scarcely reaching the shores and making no impression upon it. But on my ear they sounded like words interjected with soft laughter. There I made acquaintance with the earth, the waters, the shadows of the sky, trying often to sink my hook to the edge of a cloud. It was not in the heavens that I first noticed the stars, but their trembling images in water.

Thus by the humble and narrow environment of my childhood was it made doubly dear to me; the very limitations themselves enforcing and promoting the growth of wonder and healthy imagination. It is this which has kept alive my early memories and made them pleasant and suggestive throughout my life. Nor do I think my experiences peculiar. Sir Henry Wotton in the last years of his life happily expressed the feeling common to men. "Seeing that very place where I sat when I was a boy occasioned me to remember those very thoughts of my youth which then possessed me; sweet thoughts indeed, that promised my growing years numerous pleasures without mixture of cares; and those to be enjoyed when time, which I therefore thought slow-paced had changed my youth into manhood".

As I have already said unchangeableness is the characteristic of Bellingham, and I repeat it, that I may add that it is the counterpart of something in myself. I have been swept on with my race and my time and while sharing all their tendencies, at heart what I value most, that which is most native and dearest to me is the simple undisturbed life, full of friendliness, piety and humble amusements into which I was born. What this life was, as reflected in a happy childhood, a neglected youth and idealised by its irrecoverable loss the following pages attempt to portray.

THE WALLS OF THE WORLD

A one-storied house was lofty and convenient enough in a land where God had planted a community of his common people. That was the height of the temple of the Greeks, which was only the enlarged form of the hut or the house of their Pelasgian ancestors. It was built low in due reverence to its origin and to their gods. No other architecture has ever surpassed its beauty and sublimity. The earth is ours to build upon and over, nor much above. The early New England farmhouse was as beautiful in its place as the Greek temple. Sometimes it was set directly on the highway; sometimes in the middle of a field or on the side of rising ground, and not infrequently on the top of a hill, where it shared without deforming, the natural elevation of the earth. It was usually square, but sheds and outbuildings lengthened its appearance and these latter added a comfortable and homelike aspect and were a larger sort of window through which the wayfarer seemed to behold the life of the family more intimately. The pitch of the roof was flattened, the better to resist wind and storm, and through it arose the chimney stack. On either side of the front door were the parlor and living room; the former seldom opened, and the latter rarely occupied until afternoon and evening. The back door was the most in use at all times, and it was through it that one came nearest to the hearts and homelife of the inmates. The kitchen was where the meals were cooked and eaten, the Bible read at morning and evening and pipes lighted by a live coal from the hearth. This live coal was sometimes lost and the tinderbox missing; then the man of the family would travel to the nearest house for a spark with which to kindle his lost fire. The methods of carrying and keeping it alive were numerous and ingenious; a warming pan or iron pot would answer, if the distance was not too great. One of my forefathers awoke on a winter morning to find the ashes in the fireplace cold, and the nearest neighbor eight miles away. It was an impossible undertaking to keep a coal alive on a walk of eight miles. Wrapping a piece of cotton cloth tightly about a small stick he ignited one end at his neighbor's hearth, and like an humble Prometheus carried the smouldering gift to his little world and its belated breakfast.

The kitchen was the favorite gathering place of humble New England families and it was there they were best seen and understood; there the spinning wheel hummed while the pot was boiling or the bannock baking; there stockings and boots were dried by the open fire and the latter daily greased. With what pride did I see my first pair standing there shining in their coat of pig's scrotum, this being thought invulnerable to wet, especially snow water. Hardly could I go to bed for longing to look at them and to try them on for I know not how many times. By the wide hearth of stone or brick, one could whittle with impunity. Dirt is not common dirt in front of an open fire. Charles Lamb's clean hearth or that of the too fastidious modern house robs it of half its comfort and attractiveness. A little matter out of place, somebody's definition of dirt, is one of the most hospitable and cordial things I ever meet in the houses of my friends. A room with evidences of being lived in by the family invites me to share the intimacy of that life for the time being; but a too carefully garnished room, which my host occupies only while a guest is present, relegates me to my proper place—a stranger within the gates. It was with difficulty the family could be driven into the sitting room in the evening. The men preferred to stretch out on the settle and smoke another pipe; the boys had a little more whittling to do and loved to hear their elders talk. Rarely was an outer garment put on by men during the week days of winter except on Sundays when riding cloaks were the common wear for women, surtouts for men. These were hand woven, or if purchased, were of camlet. It was said of a certain family that a drop of its blood was as good as a great coat, so hardy and healthy were its sons.

Among such farmers and manners and customs was I born, in a red house under the great elm. In its shade the old doctor waited and talked with the expectant father until called into the house by the women who presided at such functions in the neighborhood. My memory does not reach back to the "trailing clouds of glory", but doubtless it was these which obscured the April sun that afternoon, so that the new baby could be carried out under the elm tree and there rocked to his first sleep. My next excursion, so the family traditions aver, was to Uncle Peter's, the nearest neighbor, the oracle of the community for all signs, omens and country folk-lore, who, taking me in his arms, carried me to the attic of his house and touched my head to the ridgepole: "What did you do that for?" my mother asked. "Oh, that's the way to make him a great man sometime. I does it to all the boy babies. There's luck in it." In those days there were great hopes, and prophecies had not ceased. Many a sweet sleep did I have under the elm tree's shade later on; and many a tiresome hour turning the grindstone for the long bladed sythes. In the trunk of the tree were stuck many worn out blades, their points imbedded by the tree's growth from year to year. Thus they became tallies marking the past seasons of haying. Under the tree was the afternoon parlor of the family throughout the summer; there all the feminine industries went on, braiding straw, knitting and mending, or a letter was added to the sampler. Often some neighbor came bringing her work, for nobody could be idle for a moment. I do not know what they talked about, but I can guess. However the picture is faithful and attractive, though for us, silent now. I find as few representatives of the ideal common people as of the nobility or of genius. So let them remain a picture, and do not ask for their conversation, neither for their grammar nor pronunciation. Cannot a Dorian speak Doric? Kindly and helpful neighbors can live together without the correctness and elegancies of either. To me it is hateful to see them caricatured and made literary merchandise. Not so were the classic idyls and pastorals of Theocritus, Virgil, Spenser and Saint Pierre composed. Is there nothing but bad grammar, mispronunciation and provincialisms in the heart of the rustic? Must he be forever misrepresented by his speech that he may be saved by his virtues? The closer a picture is drawn to the outward circumstance the more transient it will be. Ideals alone survive in art and literature. I should like to have the Theban law reenacted, which required the imitation in art of the beautiful and forbade the representation of the deformed and grotesque.

Four summers had passed before I knew of any world beyond the walls of the Red House, the dooryard and the shade of the elm tree. I did not feel their confinement. There seemed to be boundless liberty, and the delusion is complete when there is no sense of limitation. The goldfish in his glass prison no doubt supposes himself swimming in an infinite sea. When the boy's growth can be still measured by his mother's yardstick his outlook is restricted correspondingly. He climbs upon a chair with difficulty and cannot see over the table. This being, so lately from heaven, creeps upon the earth, and his first experiences are with the feet and under side of things. Ask the creeper how the human face, a room and its furniture appear to him. My father's face as I looked up to him seemed to be very narrow and a yard long. A face there was not. Nor had my mother's round table any top; but its two crossbars beneath, screws and catch and three feet belonged to my under world. I could explore the floor from corner to corner; the mantel-shelf, windows and ceiling were worlds and worlds above me. Lifted on some one's shoulder I touched the ceiling with my finger and knew no greater joy nor anything more wonderful.

At length the creeper raises himself to his feet. He walks, he can sit in a chair, but will not. If he only would, what care and trouble might be taken from his protectors. But he has found the door open and the alluring dangers beyond; he has found a new realm which he hears called in the homely country speech out-of-doors. There is where he now lives and finds his liveliest interests. As he is no longer a creeper but a being of importance to himself he deserves a name, and it shall be henceforth I—my own small, as yet uncapitalized i.

The walls of my newly extended world are the low enchanted hills of Mendon. There the sky seems to curve down, to rest and to end. It takes a long time to remove that horizon line; even when one is six feet, it often remains in its accustomed place. I shall pass beyond it, yet return again. My vision will be often contracted; I shall see what I once saw, become what I once was; shadowy memories become bright by the touch of hand and foot, and even the sense of smell shall guide me through many a path and restore many a room, many a threshing floor and corn crib. When thrust back upon myself, defeated, hopeless, I have retreated to the scenes of my childhood where I could be triumphant and happy in possessions, of which I cannot be deprived, and that are beyond my own power to alienate. But that time is far in the future and I am contented with the walls of my present world now expanded to the hills of Mendon. Between them and me flows the Charles stream. It is impassible as far as I can see, yet I have heard and been warned of a bridge full of peril. It is, however, an incredible distance to that bridge—as much as a quarter of a mile. When there, I dare not go forward lest I might be lost. I tremble with desire and apprehension. I return, slowly at first, then faster and faster, until, breaking into a run, I reach my mother's yard, where agitated but safe, I seem to have escaped some fearful thing. This risk gives me joy. So I go again, and this time I shall pass over the bridge and beyond into the unknown that eludes me. Adding to danger the temptation to disobedience, I go to the bridge oftener and oftener, sometimes leaning over the rail to watch for a while the chips and straws floating along the surface of the slow stream. They are moving in a direction of which I know nothing. The depth of the water at the bridge is not great, yet deep enough to be mysterious and it hypnotises me. It draws me into it and I lose myself. North and south, east and west, in the water and in the skies all is mystery which I am trying every moment to penetrate. As to myself I know nothing. Reflection, melancholy introspection, that sweet disease of youth, from which it is so difficult to escape, have not yet found me. There is as yet little consciousness of any thing beyond external and material things save a faint incommunicable magic which hangs like a veil over the bounds of a small farm. From those bounds my feet will not disengage me. On very still days I hear sounds far away and feel something within me that wishes to follow them, does indeed follow over a great space and leaves my body behind. As I hang far over the rail of the bridge I see my face in the water and become absorbed in its distorted reflections. I amuse myself exaggerating them by various grimaces, swelling out and drawing in my fat cheeks. I dare the image to battle with my little fists; it accepts the challenge and returns blow for blow.

The hither side of the bridge became more and more familiar, the farther side more and more desired. I knew the road to the school-house and to our three neighbors, all of whom I was accustomed to address as uncles and aunts. There was a fourth neighbor and nearer, yet there was a distance of some social kind. They were spoken of as Captain and Mistress Barber. To this house, a great Colonial mansion, with windows as large as those of the meeting-house, I was often sent on errands. No matter how often, I could not deliver my message, or note or borrowed salt without the greatest confusion. I felt my breath give way, something fill my throat. It was the words I was told to say over and over, repeated all the way until I was too full for utterance. Mistress Barber looked down upon me with her long white face and was able to guess the purpose of the boy's mission through his stammering and embarrassment. In her gentle, affable voice, as I now recall it, I recognise the tone of a lady. She would inquire when the errand was done if the little boy would like an apple or a cake. The question was too difficult; so she gave him both. As I turned away I passed under the great pine tree standing a little way from the mansion. It stood alone and it still stands two centuries old, in ample space and in consequence has grown symmetrical in form and luxuriant with foliage. It had realised the promise of its youth, a fate which happens to few trees in a forest. From its first majestic upward sweeping limbs to its tufted top reigned solemn and perpetual night. The wind scarcely swayed its dense and plumy branches. It merely turned up the silvery sides of the five-fingered clusters of needles which responded with a low melancholy voice like an aeolian harp, or those minor chords composed under its shade by my friend the Flute Player of Bellingham. In the woods when the pines sing it is not these I hear but the lone tree by the Barber mansion. It was the only tree in my reach I had never climbed. I was afraid of its dark mysterious recesses—also of Captain Barber.

I grew old enough to do errands at longer and longer distances. It was in doing them that I at length crossed the bridge, an event as important to the child as the Rubicon to Caesar. I began the conquest of new worlds and to beat down the Mendon ramparts. I was despatched to a more distant neighbor, the great and wealthy house of the Pennimans. In a clean frock and Sunday shoes, my face freshly washed, and with the largess of one cent with which to buy candy at the Green Store I departed full of anticipation, fear and excitement. To the bridge it was a familiar way; beyond that half a mile, never before travelled by me. I crossed the bridge with three skips and a jump; never had it seemed so narrow; but once beyond I was assailed with a thousand frights. The stone walls rose up to an intolerable height; behind them lurked innumerable wicked men and bears. There was terror in everything, and I looked back continually to see if the way of retreat remained open. When at last I lost sight of my mother's cottage my heart almost stopped beating. Should I ever find my way back? Should I ever see my home again? I hurried forward without turning my head as if the only safety now was in reaching my journey's end. Soon I climbed the eminence on which stood the Penniman mansion. Its vast size astonished me. It was two storied with a high gambrel roof making in effect a third story. Through the gambrel peaks rose two great chimneys, and I wondered what two chimneys could be for. Elaborate cornices surmounted the doors and windows; the doors were all closed, the windows draped; there was no sign of life anywhere. High shrubbery in bloom surrounded the house on three sides. There was not even a wood pile in sight, that most common accompaniment of every door yard I had ever seen. The barn and other out buildings were at some distance from the house—another strange thing. From the eminence of the Penniman mansion I could overlook the Mendon hills and to my surprise there was something beyond, indistinct, a greater distance than I had ever looked into, and there vague forms rose up, whether clouds or other hills I could not tell. My errand called me away. I lifted the heavy brass knocker of the green double door and let it fall once. It was opened and I acquitted myself very well as I did not have to speak; I had only to deliver a parcel with a note. Whether it was a lordly Penniman or only a servant who met me I knew not, as I feared to raise my eyes from under my wide brimmed straw hat, I held out the parcel, felt it taken and rushed away. Then my own important business began, the spending of my cent. The doors of the Green Store were wide open; a dog lay stretched on the platform in front; the sun poured his full rays over everything and an aspect of sleepy quiet pervaded the outside and inside of the building. There were no customers to be seen, nor sound to be heard save the buzzing of flies about the molasses measures at the farther end of the room. The store-keeper himself was fast asleep in a chair tilted against the counter. I stepped softly half fearing to awaken him. My Sunday shoes squeaked a little and the sound aroused him, though not entirely. He slowly opened his eyes, looking at me fixedly as if uncertain of any presence. Then, at length, he tilted his chair forward with a bang, put a hand on each knee, raised himself, stretched, yawned and scowled upon me as a disturber of his peace. However the trader also awoke in him and he went behind his counter. I had not yet spoken a word. Words were not necessary, for the country store-keeper knows without being told what the small urchin with one hand clutched tightly wants of him. He took down a glass jar with a bright brass cover full of sticks of candy. There was only one short question to be asked and answered, "what color"? The boy, savage that he is, knows and delights in but one, and he said "red", a word he can spell also; blue has a twist he cannot yet master. Sometime Launa's eyes are going to teach him. In the shop, as he hurried out, his eyes saw many things never seen before. He coveted them all, especially such as shone in steel or brass or bright new wood. He hardly knew their names; but what beautiful playthings they would make. All movable objects are potential playthings to him. He makes them also, like the Creator, out of nothing; if he wants a horse he has it on the instant by straddling a stick or tying a string to a companion. He has epic uses for his father's tools, his mother's knitting needles; they can slay a thousand foes at one stroke and the button bag contains them alive and dead. Six marching clothes-pins are his army and conquer the world in an afternoon.

The dog still slept as I left the store, the merchant returned to his chair, the sun shone on in noontide splendor. No shadow fell from the Penniman mansion; it looked more lifeless and larger than ever. It seemed too large to me to live in and like a meeting-house. Not a leaf stirred on the great elm; the trim spires of the Lombardy poplars had folded their limbs upward to rest, as sometimes one does his arms. The grasshopper began with a sudden shrill note which grew drowsy toward the close as if he were too lazy and hot to complete it. Over the sunburnt fields shimmered the heated air. I seemed to be the only living, moving thing; the intense hush, the high noon of the midsummer day interfused my whole being so that I hardly dared to step for fear of disturbing the universal repose. It oppressed me with a sense of loneliness. A wagon coming along the road broke the spell and all things were restored to life.

Before returning homeward I gazed once more over the Mendon hills and I wonder where and what that new looming world is. It is not many years before I know. My legs grow longer, the heart braver. I cross the bridge fearless and careless. Stone walls conceal neither friend nor foe. The forests contain only trees. I look down upon small boys; they are now my natural prey. I throw stones at them and make them cry, which gives me unspeakable delight. I am proud, restless, agitated by nameless longings. The walls of my world oppress me. Destiny has determined that I shall not be disenchanted before that world is entirely exhausted so that after many years I may recover its earliest charm. Nothing interests me more than a moment. I have become acquainted with Mistress Barber, the aristocratic Pennimans and Dr. Thurber, the poet—for Bellingham has a small poet, though I was like to forget it. He nods to me from his sulky. They say he writes his prescriptions in rhyme. He also composes epitaphs for his patients when his boluses fail to save them, and divides the glory with the local Fourth of July orators with a suitable poem. His *magnum opus* is an elementary chemistry in verse for use in schools. He had a chubby, rubicund face and a head of iron grey curls which shook as he laughed.

The Barbers and Pennimans are kind to me, but they no longer offer me an apple and a cake. Perhaps they like me and think they can make something of me. Or it may be on my mother's account, whose kind heart and sweet, winning face every body knows except herself, for she is as humble and modest as she is good. Admitted to their houses I discover new manners; their clothing is different and their rooms have unfamiliar furnishings that show no sign of usage. I sit very straight in a soft-seated chair as I have been instructed, but do not know what to do with my hands and can hardly keep them out of my pockets. My heels secretly feel for the rung of the chair; it has none, which seems curious, and it is a puzzle I take home with me. These superior neighbors of ours speak of books, of music and persons and places unknown to me. They have been as far as Mendon, beyond I imagine, for I hear the names Boston and Providence. It incites me to know all that they know, and I begin to make comparisons, to find that one house differs from another, that one person differs from another and to choose between them. All things draw or repel me. I have glimmerings of an ideal, of something less or more than is present and actual. A cent, that formerly made me rich, now makes me poor. I am not so eager for playmates; there are moments when they seem mere babies, and our sports dull and trivial. The sweet child whose frock falls only to her knees, whose wide white pantalets almost touch her red shoes, with whom I have romped for three summers alternately teasing and caressing, yet always with the lofty port of protection and superiority, no longer satisfies my heart or gratifies my pride. I try to avoid her. She follows me about meekly, confused by my coldness. Her long-lashed eyes look at me distrustfully and are suffused with tears when I decline to play. What do I care? My heart is harder than a stone. Moreover, I have transferred my affections; I am in love with a woman of twenty-three, seventeen years older than myself. To be with her makes me perfectly happy; I am transformed, I am humble to slavishness and my manner toward this enchanting being is precisely like that of my discarded maid toward me. Thus is she avenged, for I too have to suffer when unnoticed. My new love's smile, (for she only deigns to smile upon me and seldom speaks), enthralls me, I cannot express myself; I follow her about like a dog.

There is a plant called Boy Love because it never comes to fruition, seldom blooms. It is almost extinct save in old neglected house-yards. My gardener allows me to cultivate it in an uncherished corner of one of her beds. I can never pass it without plucking a spray of its fragrant leaves. Its very smell is of other days and ancient gardens. The fashionable rose cannot endure it. I mean sometime to disprove its impotence and entice it into flowering for the encouragement of little boy lovers that they be not ashamed of their infantile, ardent attachments but bravely confess them as I do.

This phase of young life passes like so many others. How swiftly they pass! and must, since we have in ten years to rehearse all the parts for the next fifty. In due time my girl playmate and also the young woman were married, and meeting long afterward we found nothing in common, not even a memory. One had forgotten that we ever played together; the other laughed incredulously at the boyish attachment. At length I too forget these mere matrons; I remember only the little maid and the coquette of twenty-three.

As one climbs the sides of a mountain it lowers its crest, but the view becomes extended. The hills of Mendon diminished as often as I climbed other hills or succeeded in reaching the topmost spires of taller trees. They were no longer so lofty, so distant, so infatuating. The walls of my world were expanded on two sides, the south and the west. All unknown lands were on the north. China was there, which to me was a place where they did nothing but fly kites; so much I remembered from my geography book; there too was Boston, merely a place where we sold our huckleberries in summer. I had been as far as Mendon and found that the world did not end there, nor were there any hills even. They had moved themselves to the next horizon whitherto my fancies had flown. Disillusions increased with my height. A yardstick no longer measured to the top of my head; the score is now marked upon the jambs of the cellar door, and sometimes I cheat with yarn balls in the heels of my boots. I cannot grow fast enough to keep pace with my ambition. When I am larger, when I am a man, then I shall— could one but recover the predicate of those phrases! There is a cell in my brain as yet filled with nothing; but there is commotion, an eddy, like that of the vorticel which is drawing thither its destined deposits. The things that draw me are also themselves moving toward me. The cell is in time filled, emptied and filled again and again. Particles of this and that remain. Who can predict what will be the permanent deposit?

The Mendon hills and those, rising continually beyond, caused me many a heart break, many disillusions, journeyings, pathless and lampless, many apprenticeships to unprofitable masters. I explored the unknown because it was unknown and because I knew not what I wanted. There was disappointment wherever the pursuit ended. I would go on—never arriving. "Stay, thou art so fair", is not the wish of boys. The mountains were not so high, the ocean not so vast, the cities not so immense, no good so good as anticipated. My heart hungered for the impossible before it had attained the possible; for the fruitage of things before the plough and the hardened hand; in fine, before reckoning with those forces which determine the happiness and miseries of life. But there is compensation for every disappointment and mistaken dream of childhood and youth. I cherish them fondly as the early drama of my life, in which, now a spectator, I see the small actor performing his mimic part with mingled feelings of amusement, censure or sympathy. When the curtain rises I am once more on my own side of the Mendon hills: the walls of that first world enclose and protect me. Here I again recover my first sense of nature and the existence of other beings; here I discern the inward foreshadowings of what was to attract and mould me through life.

SHADOWS AND ECHOES

Two things in nature impressed me more than any others in my childhood. One was the apparent motion of the moon, when I tried to walk or run away from it. To see it keep an equal pace with me, moving when I moved, stopping when I stopped, sometimes vexed me and more often amused me. The heavens are young when we are, close and companionable; they come down to the earth not more than two miles from where we stand. I tried many experiments with the moon, when it was full, to see if I could not outrun the bright and tricksy traveller. My efforts were vain and only increased my wonder. I never spoke of it nor required an explanation from my elders. Children ask no questions regarding those simple operations of nature which they first observe. They remain deep in their silent consciousness. Such as they do ask are superficial, and are either a passing impulse of a dawning social nature or are inspired by parents and teachers. I have observed that when they ask these questions they care nothing and remember naught of the answers. What is deepest in them is growing in silence; it is not yet formed into conceptions, and has no language. The difference between the spoken questions of children and their impressions, as yet so undefined, is like that between pictures of the snapshot camera and the astronomer's plates which, for hours, gather and develop the figure of some distant, unseen star.

My other childish observation was of shadows, especially my own, cast upon the ground by a low afternoon sun. This never vexed or puzzled me as did the outfooting moon. An old play says that the shadows of things are better than the things themselves; and Pindar places man at two removes from them. But indeed shadows pleased me before I knew of the humiliating comparisons poets and prophets had made; and sometimes more than the real substances with which I was familiar—trees, brooks and pastures. In the shadow of myself were the flattering length and size which I coveted, the huge man; for I wished above all other things to become a man as fast as possible that I might do and have the things which men do and have. These as I remember were trousers, long-legged boots, two pieces of pie, to sit up in the evening and never to go to school again; for I was always driven to bed and went unwillingly to my books. Many were the subterfuges by which I escaped my lessons, a lost book or a headache; and how I rejoiced in the storms which made it impossible to send me the long mile through snow or rain. I remember only one evening when I was allowed to sit up as long as I wished, my parents, having gone to see a man hung in Dedham, one of the festive occasions in old Norfolk County, the boy was left in charge of a sister. I remember it chiefly because my sister read to me that evening John Gilpin's Ride. It was the first, and for a long time, the only poem in which I took any interest. Gilpin on his horse, his cloak and bottles twain visualized themselves before me so clearly that they still remain more vivid than what I read yesterday.

But my shadow, ah, that was quite enough to satisfy my most ardent longings. Moreover I seemed able to step on it, to lengthen or shorten it, to make it assume strange grotesque shapes; in a word I could play with it. This I could not do with such objects as trees, house, barn and fences; or rather there was no such response from them as from the shadow.

Echo was the only other direct responsive thing I found in nature as yet. Echo is the shadow of sound. Echo and shadow are brother and sister; irresponsible children of nature who love to sport and play pranks with matter and make men doubt their own senses. I knew several of the dwelling places of echo; one in chief was between a large barn and a deep wood, and others at different points on Beaver Pond. Never would they return the individual voice; all came reflected back as echo's own, neither mine nor that of my companions; only now louder or less, more distinct or faint. It had a lonely, plaintive, even melancholy tone, which the Greeks explained was in consequence of an unfortunate love affair with the beautiful Narcissus. It sulked, and hiding in a cave, never spoke again unless first spoken to. I could hardly believe that echo was not the voice of a human being. To satisfy myself I examined the barn and forest for some mocking man or boy. Was not this better than the explanations which never explain to children? And who can expound a shadow? When I once heard a minister exclaim that man is but a shadow I understood him literally and was glad in my little heart thinking only of its size and nimble movements.

Echo and shadow hint of other things in nature besides solid matter and that which can be appropriated by any machinery or resolved by any chemical yet discovered. These and sounds and perfumes also remind us that the world was made for admiration and amusement as well as for use. I believe that the Creator was thinking, when He planned it, as much of little boys and girls and poets as of the husbandman and craftsman. Echo loves to imitate our voice as much as we love to hear it; and shadows love to caricature our forms that we may laugh and even assist them; for if you stretch an arm between the sun and a snowbank shadow aids you with its comic pencil. It is no wonder the sad ghosts throw no shadow; there must be sunshine, life and joy or you cannot even living cast a pleasant one. I sometimes more admire the shadows in a painting than the figures or the scene. The imperfect landscape of the Greeks excused itself from observing none in the sacred enclosures of the temples of Zeus. The light must find no impediment in the unsubstantial matter of divine beings.

It was pleasant in my afternoon rambles to see my form projected over places where I could not follow; on the other shore of a stream and along stony fields good for nothing but a crop of shadows. Thus by my shadow I triumphed over space, and when it came to a vanishing point, I imagined it still extending itself to some neighbor's door or into the next town. My eyes could not follow it nor my feet; yet something in me accompanied it and gave me a sense of magic power. An unconscious feeling for beauty in things of earth began to draw me away from houses and children and to make me lonely. I found playthings I could not carry in my pocket. These have remained with me all my life. The path we leave behind us is the one we oftenest tread. One little brook still flows through my heart. I feel it, I hear its smothered ripple, not meant for hearing, and I smell its meadowy fragrance.

I treated matter with the perfect frankness and credulity which passes away with childhood; and she rewarded me with visions and illusions that are withheld from self-guarded and discreet manhood. I knew not then that shadows were the scoffing synonym for all unsubstantial vanities and day-dreams, or that other mystic conception that substance itself is but the shadow and reflection of the power which created it, or that light itself is but the adumbration of God. How good it is that the child is ignorant of so many things. It leaves room for the existence and growth of a mind, of an imagination which, in time, shall lead rather than follow the processes of reason; which shall leap before it looks, conscious of prescience before proof, arriving on wings while the shoestrings are being tied. Blessed are the ignorance, the beliefs and the innocency of the country boy. For if he can maintain a remnant of these into maturity the world will be more beautiful; he will idealize his friends and lovers, and never be conquered by the untoward circumstances and events of his life. The child is a plant that blossoms first at the root underground, like the fringed polygala, and only after a free and natural nurture, again blossoms at the top with the same color, the same modest beauty. Let the child pursue shadows and believe them real; let him discover their unreality and suffer defeats; but he shall not know when he is defeated, for still other shadows shall allure him to the end of his days. The pursuit, not the attainment, is the true joy of living. Perilous are the conditions of attainment. The goal is seldom in sight. We are driven on from dream to dream, and to awake is to lose the charm of existence. No pearl grows in the shell without the pressure of some irritating substance; and no boy becomes a man until he has felt the sting of opposition, discouragement, defeat, and has pursued shadows with an unfaltering faith.

SHADOWS

Phantom of being, Protean face,
Parasite of rock, of towers and man
Since sun and matter erst began,
Fleet vanisher from our embrace,
Thy fairy forms the faithful ape
Of substance; all the landscape
In thy mimic loom mere woven air
Where naught is real yet all is fair;
Taunting us with bold mockeries
And willing cheats and splendid lies,
Deceiving all sense save the eyes.
Flying without wings
Gigantic o'er the mountain's knees;
Or of tiniest things
Etching their wavy images;
Or playing some fantastic trick
To please the fancy of a child;
Or tireless watcher of the sick
When others are by sleep beguiled.
Thou follower of sun and moon,
Gatherer of the undulating mass
Through which no light may pass,
Over the whole world darkening soon,
Or standing steadfast all an afternoon
Behind some oak tree's ancient crown
Until the lingered sun goes down—
Give to the weary traveller repose
In thy cool umbrageous tent,

And to the husbandman, who goes
To thee by heat and toil forespent,
Give sleep, and let thy veil his limbs enclose.

ECHO

Echo is mate of shadow and of shade,
 Saying only what is given it to say;
Hiding in wall or cave or wooded glade,
 Without ideas, sound with sound at play.

But thou, sweet echo, art my faithful friend;
 For when my simple songs on all ears die
Thou art responsive to the very end,
 And answerest them with perfect flattery.

HOLIDAYS

In the small towns of Norfolk County, even as late as the middle of the nineteenth century, Christmas was not kept as a holiday. The people adhered mainly to the Congregational and Baptist faiths. Christmas was in some way associated with Popish superstitions. The Woman in Scarlet was still preached against and feared as became the sons and daughters of the Puritans. I have never forgotten my childish vision of this wonderful creature, a vision that connected itself with a neighbor's daughter who dressed in bright red mousseline-delaine and wore an immense hoop, played the fiddle and scandalized the community by her manners, music and muslin. But the young men were all in love with her and she held a nightly court in a little brown house in that part of the town called Hard Scrabble. She took the pick of her admirers, was married at eighteen, bore what Aeschylus calls the "divine load" in fifteen travails, fourteen sons and one daughter, and lived to play her fiddle to more than thirty grandchildren. The community at length became reconciled to her, although she continued to wear to the end of her life red gowns and a bulging hoop—the women gossips now said to conceal her usual condition. To me she was and is the Scarlet Woman, an inhabitant not of Rome or Babylon, but of a town where I am the supreme pontiff, a town not made of galvanized iron nor stone nor brick, but weather-stained boards with sometimes a touch of red paint.

Doubtless many people sigh for the days when Christmas was not, for it has become a burden in its secular observances, a game of give and take. I never heard of the day in my childhood. Scarcely will this be believed, so difficult is it to realise that a present universal custom, and one so linked with religious sentiment, has not always existed; nevertheless it is true. If I were relating something that happened yesterday, or the day before, I should not be much chagrined to be disputed and to find myself in error; but the memory of the events of childhood is authentic and indisputable. There was no Christmas for children in Bellingham, or I should remember it as vividly as I do Fast Day, Thanksgiving, Fourth of July and Town Meeting Day. The last named was the first holiday of the year for the male population, occurring on the first Tuesday in March. It was a day when the solid men of the town came to the front and sat in high seats, dignified and important; when the less solid or more gay got drunk, and the boys played games about the town-house, and ate as many buns as they had cents to buy. The town-house of Bellingham was an old Universalist church whose society had been uprooted and driven away by the sermons, prayers and persecutions of the Baptist brethren and sisters. It must have been an ancient building as it had a high pulpit, a sounding board still higher and square pews. I used to go in when hungry to buy the buns, which were on sale in one of these square pews fitted up as a small shop, boards being laid on the top rail, and the high seats forming shelves for the display of eatables. I recall only the buns with distinctness, buns with three large plums sticking out of their shiny red tops, which afforded the greatest return to a hungry boy for the trifling sum he had to expend. These plums deceived me into the belief that there were more inside and sometimes I did find one lost in the air holes of the sponge-like cake. But the bun was sweet and that was enough, sweetened with white sugar too, a rare flavor in those days. I write white sugar but its current name was loaf sugar. It came in cone-shaped packages wrapped in heavy chocolate colored paper, and this paper was used by women for dyeing. These packages were hung up over the counters of all country stores. The sale was small as it was expensive and limited in use, chiefly to the sick room, wedding and funeral feasts. A trader would buy enough to last him for a long time; consequently the packages hung in their places year after year, becoming dirty and fly specked. But the inside was well protected with soft white paper, and, when opened, revealed its dazzling crystals. I liked it almost as much as candy and I rarely had a bit of the precious article. Brown sugar and molasses were the common household sweets; bread and molasses an excellent lunch for hungry boys always crying for something to eat and never filled.

The town meeting bun is a thing of the past. When I ventured into the town house I stepped very softly and felt an exceeding awe. It was a strange sensation to be moving about among men whose legs were as long as I was tall, and, generally, as unnoticed as if I did not exist. Sometimes a kindly old man would look down, put his hand on my head and say: "You'll be a man before you know it;" or another would vary the expression with, "you'll be a man before your mother." Both meant the boy had grown since the last town meeting. I have, since those days, known town meetings from the standpoint of a man and voter and have even taken part in their counsels; yet I have had always more interest in them as an observer than as an active participant. Perhaps this was because I was not an office seeker. I have revolved schemes for town improvements a whole year and taken them into the March meeting only to have them smashed in a moment. In general at the meetings in rural districts, where there is little business to transact and the day is before them, the citizens like to hear discussion, especially if the disputants get into a passion or interject a little fun. Then everybody takes a hand and the main question is so confused and lost that even the moderator cannot restate it. Party spirit rages, old feuds come to life and men remember all the ugly doings and sayings of their neighbors and are hot to pay off old scores and get even, as they say. Suddenly, at the height of the wrangle, the whole matter is dropped, peace reigns and the regular business is resumed as if nothing had happened. These tempests clear the air for a year, and everybody is in better humor having discharged his accumulation of grudges and animosities. I have heard closer speech, more sententious, more convincing and in more direct and forcible language in town meeting than from any other forum. Men are not so much ambitious of eloquence as they are to carry their point. There is often more fun, wit and sarcasm as well as logic than goes with more pretentious and popular rostrums. When the town-meeting is abolished freedom will have lost her humble but most powerful ally. When the town grows to a city all is lost; for our freedom and individual rights depend on direct and individual participation in public affairs. Otherwise, all is compromise, averages, irresponsibility and mere chance how affairs turn out. The larger the city, the easier it is for rascals to rule.

The town meeting was succeeded in April by Fast Day, appointed always for a Thursday. For some unknown reason Thursday in New England was an almost sacred day, a sort of secular Sabbath. Thanksgiving was invariably on that day of the week; also evening prayer meetings and usually religious conventions, quarterly meetings, Sunday-school conferences and weddings. There is an ancient proverb which says "Thursday come, the week is gone;" for farmers and laboring people it was uphill to that day, and an easy and quick descent to the end of the week. By Friday, or, at least, Saturday we could go a-fishing or visiting; or to the store for some Sunday snuff, tobacco or "West Injy" goods. Work relaxed a little, the strain to finish a job was less, we went to bed and arose somewhat later. Boys were not generally compelled to attend the Fast Day religious service. It had ceased to be as strictly kept as formerly. In villages and centers of towns there was customarily a match game of ball, very unlike the present base ball. Boys played with boys and men with men. The New England bootmakers, of whom there were some in most villages, were the leaders in these games. Fast Day was above all days the established one for shooting and burning powder. Why, it would be hard to discover, as it was too late for winter game and too early for any other. However, it was fun and made men and boys jolly and important to roam through the woods and fields with a gun over the shoulder, for that was still the soldiery way of carrying it. It was more often fired at a mark than at bird or beast. Powder had to be exploded to give expression to the holiday exuberance and a noise made, game or no game. I suffered dreadfully for several years in not being able to have a gun, and my misery grew acute at the approach of Fast Day. I had to content myself with percussion caps, powder and lead cannon. The latter I made myself and when I had no lead I made them of wood. These I fired as long as the ammunition held out and then with one mighty charge I would burst them into fragments, and Fast Day was over for me.

As Fourth of July approached, my chief concern was to get possession of twenty-five cents. This was the traditional limit of a boy's spending money for that day. He must save or earn it, or expect a miracle. How to save on nothing a year was an early problem of mine; and as to earning, my services, even then, were not in demand, and I cannot remember ever to have been hired to be a good boy. My mother had a cheaper way and a more effectual. Such is the miserable history of poor boys and poor mothers. Thus it was that I rarely had the twenty-five cents; it was oftener a dime. Even that seemed large enough to fill one pocket and buy a world of things. To think over all the single articles that it would purchase was to possess them for that moment, and I never had a truer ownership in my life than that which was enjoyed in these imaginary possessions. Strangely enough, I could so feel my own what I knew the dime or the quarter would purchase, that I was content not to spend it at all. Yet a day would come when some sudden impulse or appetite would snatch it away from me; then with what penitence was I overcome; for, as soon as I had a thing in my hand it ceased to have the least value; if eaten, it did not fill me; if a plaything, I soon tired and then hated it; and only its destruction gave me one passing moment of joy.

Occasionally Fourth of July was celebrated in military fashion; the train-band marched to the music of drum and fife accompanied by a procession of urchins. The crowning exercise was the firing of a salute by the whole company. It made every boy wish to be a soldier as soon as possible. Then the muskets were stacked under a great elm tree from a limb of which swung the sign, "E. Thayer, Inn" and we all took a free drink, in consideration of the dinner which was to follow at a shilling a head.

The more common observance of the day was of a much milder character, Sunday-school picnics, in which the churches of towns near each other united. We went to Mendon, and next year Mendon came to us. These picnics consisted of a little religion, much lemonade and cake, followed next day by headache. The day ended with a thunderstorm when the picnic was in Mendon; such was the common saying. Thunder storms in the night were the dread of my mother's household, especially on the Fourth of July when already excited by the day's events. We invariably expected the end of the world so much prophesied by neighbor White. If the storm came on in the daytime the whole family went to bed and covered up their heads. For my part, I longed to be out of doors in the rain, and enjoyed nothing so much as the drops falling on my bare head, and in splashing about through the puddles with bare feet. I was exhilarated by the sound of thunder, but lightning terrified me and seemed to throw me down. It was in an August thunderstorm that my father lost his life in an attempt to save his shocks of rye from ruin, which was indeed the end of the world for his family. It was no wonder that my mother and sisters were alarmed when the black clouds and sultry air came over the Mendon hills. I was too young to heed the menace or to be reminded of the domestic catastrophe and sorrow. Nature, rain or shine, winter or summer, river, pasture, clouds, woods, flowers, berries, apples, birds, were my playthings from which I was learning to find the images and equivalents in myself. Lying on my back and watching the summer clouds race across the sky gave me my first comparison and attachment of a natural object to a conscious mental conception. I arrested those clouds in their flight across the blue, and whether they went sailing on or sank below the horizon I still saw them, and their images remained firmly fixed in my mind.

It was a rare chance when I was allowed to spend Fourth of July in Milford, the little metropolis of our region. There the celebrations were on a grander scale; the local militia company gathered to itself others from the border towns, and besides fife and drum, a whole band of music marched at the head of the companies, and a cannon on the town common saluted the Fourth of July rising and setting sun and the noon of the day. There was probably an oration in the church but I had no ear for speech when my eyes were filled with seeing; for there were shows of various kinds in booths about the common and in the town hall. How to make twenty-five cents take me into all was beyond my arithmetic; so I contented myself with spending ten cents on an exhibition of Albino children, white-haired, ivory-skinned and pink-eyed. Another ten cents admitted me to a collection of dwarfs and giants, the dwarfs mounted on the shoulders or heads of the giants. The remaining five cents let me into the best show of all, a learned pig that played cards and performed amusing tricks. For a good while I wished for nothing so much as a learned pig. But now my money was gone, and I was hungry as only a boy on a holiday can be. I had walked three miles to the town, and there were three miles now between me and my mother's cupboard. When I arrived there I feasted for the remainder of the day and went to bed still hungry. The next few days were flat and languid. In all my boyhood pleasures and excitements I suffered intensely from these reactions. I tormented the family by persistent teasings to go somewhere, or to do something. "Go play, go read your book, go see what Aunt Chloe is doing," they would say. How could I fill the void with such trivial pastimes with a Fourth of July cannon ringing in my ears and the learned pig's red eyes following me? I wanted all days to be Fourth of July, and for a while I made them so with a wooden gun, a General Washington paper chapeau and a tin pan for a brass band. At length the days gradually fell into their usual tenor and I became reconciled to such amusements and mischiefs as my two playmates, George Jennison and Harry Thurber, and myself could invent.

We now began to look forward to the time of ice and snow.

Meanwhile Thanksgiving day is near. Little as it meant to me, it was nevertheless a break in the usual order of the days. I have read many cheerful accounts of the Thanksgiving home gatherings—the feastings and the frolic in which the turkey and plum pudding appeared to be treated almost like divinities. But never did I know, in boyhood, the family reunion, the turkey or the pudding, so that these gatherings and dinners are to me pictures and I regard them as I do the feasts of Homer's heroes, pleasant to read of and to imagine. Some of our neighbors celebrated the day in the customary manner and no doubt acknowledged the goodness of the Divine Providence as enjoined by the Governor's proclamation. But the bounty of the Divine Providence never travelled by our lonely road, nor left a turkey or pudding at the door of the little Red House. Saddest of all her sad days I think my mother felt it to be, seeing the bounties and friends at the tables of others and unable to make her own worthy of the occasion. She sometimes spared an aged and unprofitable hen from her scanty flock and made us each a custard in an earthen cup. For that day she brought out her only silver, six tea spoons, and spread on her round table her only table cloth, hand-woven and white as snow. In the evening we parched corn over the hearth fire. My mother sat at one corner of the fireplace and by her side a tall light stand, her candle, her Bible and her knitting. At bedtime she read a chapter aloud, and kneeling, made a low, plaintive prayer, the burden of which was always thankfulness and trust. I remember not the words, but the tone still sounds in my ear. Thus returned from year to year my four holidays until I was old enough to find the road that led from the town and on which I now love to travel back and indulge a holiday of memories.

THE AMPUTATION

Aside from the formal and appointed holidays, the events and days that a country community most enjoyed were not numerous; yet their infrequency and unexpectedness added a certain amount of zest to its monotonous annals. A fire, an accident, a death, a raising, an engagement, a fight, a new minister, even Miss Penniman's new style of gown from Boston were not unwelcome excitements. They furnished food for talk, for wonder, discussion and scandal.

Although there was a certain terror connected with the unusual event I am about to describe, yet this did not deter me from looking forward to it as a kind of holiday.

For a long time it had been rumored that our neighbor, Amos Partridge, would have to lose his leg. He had what was called a white swelling on his knee. Besides his house, Amos Partridge had a large barn and a shop, where, in winter, he bottomed boots. The bottomer of boots sat on a low bench and did most of his work on his lap and knee. It was thought that the primary cause of Amos' trouble arose from a slight blow upon his knee as he sat at his work, increased by subsequent constant pressure upon the spot by the strap which held the boot in place. He worked as long as he was able, and for some time before the operation, he was obliged to use a crutch in passing from his shop to his house. The swelling grew steadily in size, and became more and more troublesome although every remedy then known to New England therapeutics had been tried, including all the nostrums of the neighborhood, plasters, poultices, washes and prayers; for Amos was much beloved by his neighbors, mostly Methodists, to which sect he himself belonged. He was about thirty-five years old, tall and large-framed, light-haired, full-bearded and with blue eyes, a pure Saxon type of a man. His forehead was high and narrow and much work and suffering had ploughed untimely furrows upon it. His house stood close by the roadside, in a field between two pieces of woodland. It was small, one-storied, the only unusual thing about it being that it was painted white, as was also the neat fence which enclosed a tiny space in front almost touching the road. This enclosure was in summer a tangle of cinnamon roses, lilacs, sweet-william, bouncing-Bet and other common flowers which propagate and harvest themselves. A narrow gravelled walk, upon which the flowers constantly encroached, led to the front door—a useless door, generally, as no one ever thought of entering it. There were two rooms on either side of this door; one, the family sitting room, the other, the sacred country parlor with the usual hair-cloth covered furniture and home-made rugs in bright colors and quaint patterns. There was a gilt mirror too, the upper third of which was opaque, and upon it was painted a one-masted vessel with impossible sails set straight from stem to stern, which helps me to recall the room and much of the interior of the house. I had never seen so fine a picture; nor had I ever seen a vessel of any kind. It was wonderful. I never tired of looking at it although I had seen it many times as the room was opened for prayer meetings, which my mother attended regularly, taking me with her. How well I recall those meetings, which sobered me for life. Not that any spoken words impressed me, for I understood nothing of what was said or sung; but there was a sadness, a suppression in the air, as of the valley of Jehosaphat. The stillness too, that intense hush which often occurred between the remarks and prayers of the brethren and sisters, filled me with a nameless, shrinking fear. Had I been old enough, conversion would have been easy as the only means of escape from those terrible silences. My usual relief was in clinging to my mother's hand which gave me a sense of protection from I knew not what; or in looking at the vessel in the mirror and sailing away to other worlds.

Under that sail I visited all the neighboring inland towns whose names and nothing more I knew—Milford, Medway, Mendon and Hopkinton, the utmost bound of my little world—beyond Hopkinton, nothing.

At length there came a day when Amos Partridge could work no longer; the pain in his knee became too excruciating to be endured. The surgeon was summoned and a date determined for an amputation. The neighborhood was informed and nothing else was talked or thought of during the preceding days. The chances of Amos surviving the operation were discussed; for it was before the days of anaesthetics and the science of surgery had not then made the removal of a limb the least of its triumphs. Most of the neighbors, especially the women, took a hopeless view of the result. Preparations were made much resembling those for a funeral. My mother told me she was going to the amputation, and as she never left me at home when she went abroad, I knew I should go too. But this did not oppress me, not nearly as much as the thought of a prayer meeting. A dim sensation of something extraordinary about to happen filled me with excitement. Yet, on the whole, it was an emotion of joy.

The momentous day of the amputation arrived. I could hardly restrain my impatience. It was a calm, soft afternoon in early spring when my mother and I set out for the house of Amos Partridge; not however, before my mother had been to her chamber, and, on her knees, offered a silent prayer. She appeared very serious and silent on the way. Could she be ignorant of the pleasure I was anticipating? I danced along by her side; hardly feeling the earth beneath my feet; I was already at the scene of expected festivity. I noticed that my mother carried a fan. It was not a hot day and I wondered much what the fan was for. We arrived at the house where there was already a considerable assemblage of the neighbors and friends from a distance. Horses were fastened to trees, fences and the sides of the barn, just as on Sunday at the meeting-house or at the annual town-meeting. The small boy was there in numbers, but only a few girls. Alas, for the small boy! He was not permitted to play near the house nor to make the least noise. Instead of a holiday, for him, it turned out a more serious affair than the usual Puritan Sabbath. Bitter was my disappointment. My mother, as she left me to go into the house, warned me to keep very still and be a good boy. Accordingly I remained under the window of the room in which the operation was to be performed. The windows were wide open, and I could see and hear all that was said and done. I had a view of my mother and two other women standing by the bedside of Amos, fanning him. I could see the face of the sufferer, pale, emaciated and troubled. Presently I heard the voice of the minister, and looking toward the foot of the bed, I saw opened before him the great family Bible from which he was reading. From the frequent recurrence of the words boils and afflictions I think it must have been some chapter in Job that he had selected as suitable for the occasion. After the Scriptures the minister made a long prayer.

Then the dreadful preparations began. I saw the bed-clothing pulled back and the diseased limb exposed; it was twice its natural size. The surgeon was the once famous Dr. Miller, of Franklin, reputed the seventh son of a seventh son, some extraordinary gift in surgery being credited to such a descent. In his day he performed all the surgical operations in that part of Massachusetts and the bordering towns of Rhode Island. Spread out on a small table at his right hand were his instruments, whose names I did not know, but they interested me immensely. What would I not have given for one of those dainty polished saws or keen knives with handsome handles! The room was partly filled with neighbors, mostly women, ready to lend their aid to the surgeon and to comfort the patient, whose family sat weeping in an adjoining room. Amos' eyes were now closed and his mouth set firm. As the tourniquet was twisted tighter and tighter the lines in his brow grew deeper. He breathed hard and a moan, the only one, escaped him as the knife went through the outer skin. It was not long before the sound of the saw came through the open window. The operation was over and the leg had taken its last step with its fellow. It was carried away into the barn for dissection; we heard with awe that Amos felt a faint sensation of pain when the knives and probes were searching for the hidden disease, as if the severed limb still remembered its possessor.

Subsequently the remains of the leg were buried in Amos' garden, which gave rise to some questionings in this pious and scrupulous community as to whether it ought not to have been placed in the graveyard. But Amos said that he did not own a lot yet, and when he died, he should not need his old leg to welcome him to his grave

The operation proved successful. In a short time Amos was up with the empty pantaloon fastened back and the stump of the leg encased in a thick leather protector. As he had used crutches for some time before the amputation he soon learned to accommodate himself to their new use. He could not now walk long distances, so the weekly prayer meetings were generally appointed at his house. He became what was called among Methodists a class-leader; he took the leading part in all the private religious gatherings and never failed in his opening prayer to thank the Lord for bringing him safely through his peril. "It was Thy hand that held the knife", he would exclaim, "yea, it was"; and all the brethren said, amen.

There was, in the little community of which Amos Partridge was the central and pathetic figure, a sincere belief in the nearness and activity of Heaven in its every day affairs. It rendered them serious, careful and slightly superstitious. It was also true, however, that these tendencies sometimes seemed to create antagonism and a rebellious spirit in the young men. We children, from the same causes, were timid, afraid of the dark, afraid of everything; or, it may be, these very, nameless terrors of the night, of wild beasts and the forests, together with reactions from fancied escapes were the best stimulants and rustic guardians of the imagination—the primitive Muses of the Bellingham boy.

COUNTRY FUNERALS

If a surgical operation brought with it a country lad's holiday, a funeral may also be reckoned among the events which varied his life, if not with gaiety, at least with pleasing diversion. As a very young child I was present at two funerals which for special reasons have impressed themselves upon my memory. I had heard much of a widowed sister of my father, supposed to be rich; this proved to be a fable. Her husband had left the bulk of his estate to foreign missions, and only a bare support to his wife. As he had acquired his property by selling liquor it was but natural he should wish to make a restitution in the land of the heathen. The widow, my aunt, lived to an advanced age. When she died I accompanied my family to her obsequies. There I met her other young nephews and nieces besides the children of the neighborhood. We had a merry time together all day except for the hour of the services. There was a general feast served for everybody. The children were served at a second table, but there was a plentiful supply of goodies reserved for us and no tears to check our appetites. At the table we were told that our aunt had left us each fifty dollars. I had never heard of, least of all, seen such a sum of money and I conjectured it was enough to last the remainder of our lives.

A great deal takes place at a country funeral characteristic of the kindly as well as the weaker side of rustic men and women. There is much bustle and subdued cheerfulness mingled with awe; conversation is carried on in whispers. The chief mourners are permitted to be as helpless as they please; everything is done for them; they are treated as automatons.

They are arranged in ranks next to the corpse according to consanguinity. Then come the neighbors and those persons who love to attend funerals. Children bring up the rear and in the hall and doorway lean a few men who seem to have no particular relation to the occasion. The important personage, not excepting the minister, is the volunteer undertaker, who for some unknown reason, has become the man usually called upon to officiate at the exercises. He knows his business, and for an hour feels himself a man of consequence. He is impartial in his attentions; be the dead old or young, saint or sinner, he is equally anxious that the ceremonies shall be conducted with proper decency and order. The rich give him a little more care, as they, perhaps, have rendered unto their dead a handsomer outfit for their last appearance and farewell journey; such I think may have been the case when our distinguished neighbors, the Scammels and Pennimans passed away. When the minister has concluded his remarks and his prayer, generally in the most lugubrious words and scriptural phrases he can muster, the man in charge of the funeral, (for country people knew no such professional name as undertaker), comes briskly forward, and, with much ceremony, lifts the lid of the coffin, rearranges some portion of the dress about the face of the dead, gives a searching glance over the coffin and then announces: "The friends and all those who desire, may now view the 'remains'". This is the most affecting moment in the ceremony; the last parting look which wrings the heart of the stoutest, when the women break down and are led away blinded by their tears. It is then that the most indifferent spectator pays that beautiful tribute of weeping for those he may not have loved, nay, hated or despised. All the ill is forgotten, the good alone remembered. A hearse was hardly known in the old days. The coffin was placed on a bier of home construction and carried to the graveyard on the shoulders of four men. The sad funeral procession followed behind, the mourners walking two and two and the rear made up of a straggling company of men, women and children. The minister offered a farewell prayer at the grave, and in summer time, an appropriate hymn was sung, its appropriateness consisting mostly in its dismal words and tune. Then the terrible moment arrived, the lowering of the coffin and the sound of the first earth upon it; for, formerly the company awaited this last act. This was not the formal dust to dust, a verbal and figurative act, but some shovelfuls of real earth that for a few moments rattled and pounded the top of the coffin with a heart-rending sound. The minister shook hands with the chief mourners, every one took his way home, the bier was placed under a tree and left to the elements and to be the plaything of boys until the feet of them, that await at the door to carry out the dead, are heard again.

The next funeral of which I have a recollection came into my own home. My father was dead, dead in the prime of his life, his labors and his hopes. Of this event I recall only two things, being taken from my playthings under an apple tree to the grave, and the hard pressure of my hand by my sister as the coffin was lowered. This became in after years my most pathetic memory as I grew to realize what it meant. In that grave all our hopes were buried; that I was unconscious of it must have made the grief of my family only the more poignant. At the same time I became the object of their greater solicitude and affection, and it was a miracle that, in a family of women only, I was not spoilt by too much indulgence. But while my sisters petted and pampered me, my mother's graver manners and prayers doubtless saved me from being too selfish and effeminate. Boys, however, owe chiefly to each other their escape from the apron string and the softness of nursery manners.

How empty now seemed the house whence the dear father had gone forever. The problems of life offered themselves to my mother and sisters with a terrible and crushing reality. My sisters were old enough and had sufficient education to teach the summer terms of district schools. My mother boarded the winter schoolmaster and planted and cared for her garden with her own hands. There was a pig in the pen and a flock of hens in the sod house. Most of my father's tools were sold at public vendue, which brought in a little ready money. There was straw to be braided at one and a half, sometimes two cents per yard; in summer huckleberries were picked and sold for three and four cents a quart. There was a peddler who made his rounds monthly and always put up for the night at my mother's house, paying his score with a liberal barter of such articles as he carried, dry goods, women's shoes and small wares. Dresses were made over and over, were darned and patched as long as the cloth would hold the stitches. My father's clothes were cut down for me and I wore the last of them in my sixteenth year. My straw hats and winter caps were home-made. Every year a cousin in business in Woonsocket Falls presented me with a pair of new boots. There was no want in the household because wants were few and had been reduced to the last limit. I am sure I never went cold or hungry although I never had a boughten plaything or any of those delicacies which are more necessary to children than necessities.

It is in such circumstances that the friendliness of country neighbors appears in its most beautiful light. There is no thought of almsgiving on their part, nor a sense of accepting charity on the part of the recipients. Benevolence and gratitude were not called upon to exchange compliments. Farmer Bosworth is going our way and leaves a jug of milk; he stops to chat a while and relight his pipe with a coal from the hearth. Would you see him do it with a boy's eyes? The tongs are too long and heavy to bring around to his pipe; but with them he pulls out a coal of the right size, picks it up between thumb and finger and puts it into his pipe bowl. I stand close beside him, and although he doesn't cringe, I do, and almost feel my fingers burn. He winks out of the corner of his eye at me and says, 'Your old daddy is tough isn't he?' and shows me the end of his thumb calloused and hard as the knurl of white oak; only fire could clean it to the original skin. He shakes out his blue frock for fear of fire in it, and goes his way. There is always something to spare by those who have more, to those who have less. Whoever kills a fatted cow or a pig in early winter sends a portion to the Red House; and a load of wood is left in the night by some farmer who does not wish his right hand to know what his left doeth. Money is scarce; but everything else is shared with those in distress or in sickness. This is so much a matter of course that no one thinks of credit or reward.

In such ways as I have described were the widow and her fatherless children saved from destitution or loss of their respectable position in the little community. I am sure my mother relied with complete trust on the scriptural promises made to those in her difficult circumstances. If they were fulfilled by human agencies, that, also, was the doing of the Divine Director of the affairs of the poor. In those days men and women were good and simple, obedient, not only unto the commands and examples of their Bible, but also to the impulses of their own kind hearts.

Yet the household never again felt the highest happiness of domestic life. A soft and tranquil resignation took its place. They moved about with a gentler step, speaking in subdued tones, more often not at all. They had to live out their lives, although it now seemed hardly worth the struggle. Tears were in their eyes at the table, and one or another would arise before the meal was half finished. I heard suppressed sobs as I went to sleep on a truckle-bed beside my mother, who during the day was more composed than her daughters. Neighbors soon began to call; there was then a hearty cry in which everybody in the room joined. Nothing so relieves the pent-up feeling as this, if only a little sympathy is present, as it were, to receive and consecrate the precious and sacred tribute of tears.

As for me when I returned from the grave of my father, unconscious of what had happened, I resumed my interrupted play under the apple tree. I had never as yet wept for anything except the crossing of my will—April tears, soon dried.

MY MOTHER'S RED CLOAK

My mother was a silent woman, seldom speaking unless first addressed, and she never asked questions of callers beyond what an extreme courtesy required. I noticed the latter trait when a child, in contrast to the custom of most people; for to ask questions seemed to be the usual and almost only manner of carrying on conversation among the neighbors. Moreover, I was myself pestered beyond endurance by a fire of questions whenever I went anywhere, or anybody came to us. I inherit from my mother a great reserve in speech and fondness for silence; and, as the latter can only be purchased by retirement, I have added to silence a love of solitude in which I have doubtless too much indulged myself. All sorts of suppositions follow a man who retires and declines the ambitions of his contemporaries. By some he is thought a coward or eccentric; by others he is believed to be a philosopher. Those of a more indulgent temper guess that delicate health or some disappointment in love, in business or profession has driven him away from his kind. None of these solutions hits the marks. And although I have no wish to relieve myself of responsibility for my course of life, still less to apologize for it, destiny, in form of a woman, my mother, has directed my life in spite of reason, the persuasion of friends or the allurements of the world—the world which inflicts its just penalties upon him who refrains from becoming an actor, who persists in being a spectator. The paradox of my nature is that I love my kind as much as I love solitude and silence. My friendships are now sixty years old. My mother also enjoyed society although she never sought it. She was easily amused, but I never heard her laugh aloud; her whole face smiled and it was more contagious than the outbursts of more demonstrative persons. She listened apparently with all her senses and faculties. It was this characteristic I imagine, that, when outward voices were withdrawn, made possible the turning of an inward ear to the responses of her soul. In no other way can I account for the fact that without education or opportunities she became a refined gentle-woman, became intelligent without books and had an insight and judgment in all matters within her sphere, much depended upon by her family and acquaintances. She was feminine to the tips of her fingers, and sympathetic with distress and misfortune. From her scanty cupboard she fed all who asked for food. She believed and often said that the loaf which is divided is never consumed. Wandering beggars knew her door and were never turned away. But, as her house was small, and without a man, if they asked for shelter, she sent them to the next neighbor.

Bred in such a quiet atmosphere I was usually very silent in my mother's presence. When alone on the road, or in the fields, or with my playthings I talked to myself a great deal; or rather I addressed inanimate objects as if they were living beings, a habit which still clings to me, although the voice is no longer needed. My days were full; I found everywhere enough to keep my feet moving and my hands busy. I was completely filled and satisfied with the earth just as I found it in the town of Bellingham. When, however, evening came on and I had to go into the house, everything shrank to the size of the room. I became restless and fretful. Having exhausted every amusement which the house afforded and, however sleepy, unwilling to go to bed, I sat down upon a cricket at my mother's knee and kept saying, "tell me one little story."

One such evening I recall when the days were growing short and shorter and the candle was lighted at half past four o'clock. It was a privilege always granted me to light the candle. If no one happened to be looking I blew it out for the pleasure of relighting it; for, like other children I loved to play with fire and the candles and the open hearth gave me ample opportunities. The bellows and I were intimate and constant playmates. We played many a trick together; sometimes stealing up behind one of my sisters and blowing into her ear, or going some distance away from the candle I made a current of air which would sway the candle flame, when my mother would exclaim, "how the wind does blow; some door must be open." Then my titter would reveal the rogue, who was reminded that it was his bedtime.

But, on the evening to which I have referred, I was a good boy having expended my naughtiness during the day. There was a still calm throughout the house and the intense cold had hushed the air over field and wood. The candle was alight on the three-footed stand and my mother was counting the stitches in the setting of a new stocking. As usual I was coaxing for a story. Perhaps it was the red yarn which reminded my mother of her red cloak, or some sudden flash of tender memories. When she had fairly started the stocking so that she could knit without counting or looking at her work she said, "I had a red cloak once; would you like to hear about it?"

"Oh yes, and tell it long, long, mother."

"I was a little girl then, so the cloak was short, and so the story. Red was the color I most admired when I was ten years old. It became me, so I thought, for I was almost as dark skinned as an Indian. Folks called me Widow Thayer's red-winged blackbird when I wore my cloak, of which I was very proud. It had no sleeves and came down to my feet and was closed at the neck with a fastening of silk cord braided in a pretty pattern.

"I went to meeting in it all one winter, proud and gay, but never wore it on any other day except the Sabbath. At the end of winter it was packed away in a great chest where our winter clothing was kept in summer with tansy laid among the garments to prevent moths. My red cloak was placed at the bottom of the chest and I myself spread an unnecessary number of green tansy sprays over it. I never thought of the cloak again until the next winter. When it was taken out for me to wear one cold November Sabbath, what was my grief to see the cloak, as I thought, ruined. The tansy leaves had printed their exact shapes in a dark brown color all over the back, which had lain uppermost in the bottom of the chest. The pressure and the heat had acted like a dye. I cried my eyes red and would not go to meeting. Every one thought the cloak was spoilt. But one day the minister's wife called at our house, and the sad tale of the cloak was related to her, and asking to see it she said, "Why, if it wasn't pretty before—and I never liked red for little girls—it certainly is now. It is beautiful with those brown leaves; it looks almost like a palm-leaf cashmere shawl." Now a palm-leaf cashmere shawl was the finest and most costly outer garment a woman could possess in those days. My mother and sisters agreed with the minister's wife, as her opinion about all women's concerns was as much respected as was her husband's on religious matters. So I began to wear the cloak again, and people thought it was a new one, and wondered how my mother could be so extravagant when she was so poor. But the cloak was much admired and thought to become me more than the last year's red one. The secret was not kept long for the minister's wife explained it to someone to free my mother from the charge of extravagance. Soon everybody knew it and many inquiries were made how it happened. Some of our neighbor's daughters even tried to produce the same effects on their dresses and cloaks by pressing green leaves on them with hot flatirons. But it did not succeed. You cannot imitate accidents; they just happen once; the next one is something different. So all the girls envied me my cloak. It lasted me ten years, for I was not much taller at twenty than at ten."

My mother was silent again and I exclaimed "is that all, mother? Tell some more, do."

"Stories, my son, must have an end or you would not like them—but there would never be another. I have heard of a book that had a thousand, but it took a thousand evenings to tell them. So one an evening ought to be enough, and it is your bedtime."

Here my youngest sister, Harriet, who was fifteen years old, said, "Mother, why don't you tell him the other part of the cloak story?"

"Yes, tell it," I entreated.

My mother appeared to be wholly absorbed in her stocking; she had dropped a stitch and was working her needles painfully, trying to recover it. A half sad smile, half pleased expression came into her face and a faint blush upon her brown cheek.

"Well, I suppose the journey I took in the red cloak with the tansy figures is what your sister wants me to tell you about. My mother, your grandmother, was a widow. I never saw my own father, for I was born while he was away fighting in the battles of the Revolution and he never returned; he was killed at Yorktown. When I was about ten years old my mother had an offer of marriage from a farmer in Medway who had lost his wife; his children had grown up, married and settled excepting one son twenty years old. It was a matter of convenience on both sides; my mother needed a home and he needed a housekeeper. The marriage took place in her own house. But she did not go immediately to her new home; she had a little property to dispose of and other small affairs to arrange. When she had sold everything but her old white mare she set out for Medway upon the mare's back, taking me with her on a pillion behind. It was a day in Spring, and although not cold, I wore my cloak as the easiest way of carrying it. No doubt it was a queer spectacle we made; yet, not as queer then as it would seem now—the old white mare ambling along, head down, and feet hardly clearing the ground under the heavy load, for your grandmother was a large, stout woman and we had a number of bags and bundles fastened onto the saddle, and I almost hidden among them, was quite covered by my cloak so that I might have been mistaken for another parcel hanging behind my mother's broad back. She wore an immense bonnet flaring wide in front and big bowed silver spectacles. I had on a small tightly-fitting bright yellow cap tied under my chin with blue ribbon. It was not a long journey from Bellingham to Medway, but it was the first I had ever taken, and it seemed to me it would never end. I was much subdued and even frightened on the way. It was all so strange and perplexing to me this marriage of my mother to a strange man, giving up my childhood home and going to another of which I knew nothing. Little did I imagine the destiny that awaited me there.

"At last we turned into a long lane and came to a large rambling farm house with barns all about it. A young man came to the doorstep to meet us. I was not in the habit of taking much notice of boys and young men, but I could not help seeing that he was a handsome youth, tall, fair haired and blue eyed. He helped my mother to dismount, and then lifted me in his arms from the pillion. That young man, my son, was your father, and I have heard him say he that moment fell in love with the little girl in the red cloak. He seemed never so much pleased as when winter came round and I began to wear it again. He waited and served ten years for me, and when I was twenty and he thirty we were married. We went back to Bellingham to be married by my mother's minister, an old friend. We went on horseback, I on a pillion behind your father just as I had left the town and wearing still my red cloak, but almost for the last time, for it was thought no longer suitable for a married woman. It was hung away in a closet; your father would not have it made over into any other kind of a garment, as was the thrifty custom of all households, although I much wanted to make it into a petticoat. Your father prized it more than any of my newer clothes, and it hung in the closet for many a year. Sometimes in the long winter evenings when we would be talking of old times and the ten tedious years of his waiting, he would make me take out the cloak and parade around the room. It seemed to make him happy and more affectionate."

MY UNCLE LYMAN

As I shall often allude to my Uncle Lyman in these pages, I will sketch as much of his character and his ways as I can now recall, and that may interest the reader. He was a farmer of the old style and I love to remember him. To hear of great men and great events is stimulating, as even the sound of fire is warming; yet the memory of those who have been near and dear to us brings a deeper glow into the heart.

Uncle Lyman's farm supplied nearly every one of his needs except what were called in his day West India goods. He believed with Cato that the father of a family ought always to sell and never to buy. He strictly followed his advice in selling his old cattle, his old carts and used up tools and everything which he did not want. This was why his yards and buildings were unincumbered with the trumpery which so often disfigures New England farms. West India goods were the luxuries of his time. These goods were chiefly rum, sugar and molasses. Tea and spices were even greater luxuries. The strange marks on tea chests were a cipher no one had unravelled. On his farm were raised corn, wheat and always rye, for rye and not wheat was in Bellingham the staff of life. Eggs, cheese, butter and pork were bartered at the country stores for West India goods. Work, incessant work was the prime necessity on the farm and in the house, and Uncle Lyman and his wife never knew an idle day. This fixed upon him a serious and preoccupied air. He began the day early and left off late. The sun was his fellow traveller and laborer to and fro in the furrow, the corn rows and the swath. But it was hard for him to leave his work at sundown; darkness alone sometimes compelled him to quit the field. After supper, which was at five o'clock, the year round, is half and the better half of the day in summer, he used to say. Our Bellingham neighbors were humble, hard working people, but they taught me "the great art of cheerful poverty." I was early cured of several follies by standing under the shadow of rustic wise men. I drove their oxen to the plow, and often fell behind alongside the ploughman and picked up the scattered seeds of old, traditional wisdom in his furrows. With these the sagacious urchin sometimes astonished his little mother. Visitors, a cloudy day, a gentle rain did not prevent Uncle Lyman from his labors. "Let us keep ahead of the weather," he would say, "and then we can go a-fishing." No weeds grew in his corn or rye; and his made hay seldom was wet. He scented a shower from as far away as the Mendon hills. He first taught me to notice the sweet perfume which a summer shower drives before it from afar, the combined perfume of wild flowers, trees and new mown grass.

There was always the promise held out that, after haying or the first hoeing, we should go a-fishing on Beaver Pond, and sometimes the promise was kept. He was a masterful trailer for pickerel; he put into it the same energy as into his axe and scythe. In the same way that I was allowed to drive his mare Nancy by holding the slack of the reins, did I have my part in the fishing excursions. I held a line over the edge of the boat until the fish bit, then another hand took it and drew it in. Perch or pout it was mine, and credit and praise were duly given. "What a smart boy!" words that made me more proud than any commendations I have heard since. When they were cooked I wanted my own catch to eat and was humored. And in general that is the boy's disposition; whatever he captures or finds on trees or on the earth he wishes to eat. No doubt a green apple and the buds of trees, and all kinds of sweet or peppery roots give him that wild and strenuous virtue which enables him to resist pampering and effeminating influences.

Although Uncle Lyman seldom allowed himself a holiday, I

believe he enjoyed it as much as I did. He was simply an older boy; that was the secret of our sympathy and my admiration for him. He knew so many more things than I, could do so many more, yet when with me, all in a playful way as if they were of no account, and only for fun. He was my model and my ideal of a man in everything that made for me the world. I felt an inward, irresistible impulsion to do all that he did, just as we are inclined to beat time to the music that we love. Thus was I taught to labor and enslaved to it before I knew it; for a boy wants to do what he sees men do; he must handle the hoe, the rake, the axe and the scythe, and these are often made to suit his size and strength in order to tempt him still further on. Thus does he forge his own chains; he is caught in his own net and his plaything tools become his masters. Now he must mow and hoe in earnest, however hot the sun, however much he hates to work. Yet I have never felt any distinction between work and play when the former was to my liking.

Uncle Lyman's wisdom had been handed down to him by his fathers, and he had improved it by observation. He added a new touch to the wrinkled face of ancient use. He knew the properties of all trees, weeds and herbs. Ash and hornbeam were his most precious woods. Ash served every purpose this side of iron; it was as good as a rope, for was not the Gordion knot tied with it? and could be whittled down as fine as a knitting needle without breaking, and still keeping its strength; it could be pounded into basket stuff, separating the layers to almost any degree of thinness. It handled every tool, from a pitchfork to an awl, and made the whole of a rake, the bows, teeth, head and staff. Besides, it had medicinal virtues; it was good for nose-bleed ever since it staunched the royal nose of King James, the Second. Although the most elastic of wood it never grew crooked, but shot up a trunk as straight as an arrow. It is a tree prophetic of archery. Uncle Lyman made me many a bow from a selected piece of ash, each year of my age a little longer and stouter. He measured the length the bow should be by my height. What a joy it was at length to shoot an arrow almost out of sight! "Now", said Uncle Lyman, "you are almost big enough for a gun". Alas, I might as well have wished for a kingdom. A wooden gun for awhile satisfied my ambition. With that, however, I shot many an Indian, and the little boys and girls who teased and provoked me. But I soon tired of these imaginary foes and marksmanship. With bow and arrow I could hit the trunk of a tree, the house door, and by accident a pane of glass. Best of all I liked to shoot over Uncle Lyman's dooryard elm, or try for the clouds. Often I lost my arrow in them; so I bragged and believed.

The hornbeam was much less common than the ash and was saved with particular care. It was mainly used for stanchions in the tie-ups of cows and oxen, for stakes on sleds and carts, and for levers. It is not easily bent and is almost impossible to break; it is the steel of the forest. Its foliage resembles that of the elm, but is finer and denser. It has no insect enemies and minds not the fiercest tempests. Uncle Lyman said only lightning could rive it, that the hornbeam drew fire from the clouds, and one should never go near it in a thunder storm. This was only when it was alive.

His various speculations about natural objects and phenomena, were always in the way of contraries and offsets. Good weather was enough to ensure forthcoming bad; a full crop this year meant a poor one next year. If every kernel of corn sprouted, look out for plenty of crows and a poor yield. Thus he comforted himself in every reverse and humbled himself in good fortune. In good years he was more saving, and in bad, less so than most of his neighbors. Now he had a fear ahead and now a hope. Thus he balanced both; yet the balance so inclined that the years increased his store, and thrift, industry and honesty brought him honor among his neighbors. He helped the widow and the orphan and loaned money without a mortgage. His debts and credits were obligations of honor; as he paid, so he was paid.

Uncle Lyman admired trees as the most wonderful things that God had made grow out of the earth. He could hardly bring himself to chop them down. The crash of a falling tree which gave me the most intense delight, made him sorrowful. He stood awhile over it as over the corpse of an old friend. He had known it for many a year, had noted its growth from a sapling to a tree as old as himself. Like the old man of Verona,

> "A neighboring wood, born with himself, he sees,
> And loves his old contemporary trees".

The trees I loved and played with most in my boyhood, the white birches, for which I still have more fondness than any other in our northern forests, Uncle Lyman cared for not at all. Although he had a sense of beauty, and long association with an object affected him with a tinge of romance and secret sentiment, yet utility was the chief criterion in his estimate of trees and men. Could you do a good day's work, it was enough; it filled the measure of a man and the promise of a boy. A useful tree was therefore the best tree. He had no use for white or gray birches, for they were neither timber nor vendible firewood. He often ridiculed them, and if there was a worthless fellow in town, he was, in his comparison, a gray birch, good for nothing but to hoop the cider barrels, of which the fellow was too fond; if a too gay girl, she was a white birch, dressed in satin, frizzled and beribboned, dress over dress of the same stuff to her innermost petticoat. He saw no good in the birch except for the backs of naughty boys. I now know a hundred uses for the birch, unsuspected by him. He had never heard of peg and spool and bobbin mills, nor of the mountain poet who makes his own birch bark books, on whose leaves he inscribes his simple songs—and, envied man, is able to sell them.

But all these useful, playful and poetic uses are nothing to me in comparison to the birchen bower wherein I spent entrancing summer days with Launa Probana.

Having been my father's most intimate friend, when he died in the midst of his years, he became my mother's adviser and helper, and to me a second father. I loved him well, and I believe he reciprocated this boyish affection. His eyes twinkled and the wrinkles on his weather-beaten face ran together when

I approached him in the field, or when we talked together beside the hearth fire or under the elm tree when the day's work was done. For some reason I cannot now fathom, unless it were the ambitious desire to put myself on a footing with his years and wisdom, I would assume with him an unnatural gravity. My wisdom consisted in asking him questions, any that happened to come into my head. I took for granted that he knew everything. Had he not been to Boston, and more than once? Yet little would he say about that town. He liked much better to talk of places he had never seen, especially London and London Bridge. I only learned that people in Boston dressed every day in the week in their best clothes; that was what made the deepest impression upon me; for our best clothes hung in the closet until Sunday. Uncle Lyman and I went barefooted and shirtsleeved all summer. He never had a linen shirt or collar; but how fine he looked in a snowy white cotton shirt and broad collar, a blue coat and tall bell-shaped hat, a hat he had worn all his life on the Sabbath and at funerals. Nor do I think he had, during his manhood, more than one best suit of clothing. In winter he always wore a long woolen frock made by his wife, and a cap of woodchuck skin. Folks said it was like to be a hard winter when he put on his overcoat. His complexion was as dark as an Indian's; eyes as black as night, and he had straight raven hair. He used much tobacco, always a quid in his mouth except when it was a pipe. He mostly refrained on the Sabbath until the evening when a long quiet smoke compensated him for abstinence during two sermons. His voice was rich and seemed to come from deep down in his chest. When he was a bit puzzled, he scratched his head with one finger. He was scrupulously neat in his person and orderly in his yard and buildings. No chips, no broken-down carts nor tools disfigured his premises. His was almost the only barn of a working farmer I ever saw that was kept clean and neat—except my own. He did not belong to any church; but he had a whole pew in the body of the meeting-house and contributed his full share to the support of the Gospel. Moreover he gave of the produce of his farm every year something to the minister's woodshed or cellar. I never heard him but once make any comment on the sermons he had heard, which were more than five thousand according to his figures. "My boy", he said to me one Sunday evening, "if you should ever be a parson, try to make your sermons different every time. It seems to me as though I had heard the same sermon all my life". On the Sabbath day, after the chores were done, there were shaving and dressing, the fires to be put out and the windows to be made fast with a button or a nail. Then the carryall was brought out, a high narrow vehicle difficult to get into, and still more difficult to get out of. The mare, Nancy, was called white, but she had patches of brown along her expansive sides and was, with much effort, squeezed between the fills, and the straps made tight in their buckles. Nancy winced at this tightening. She did not like her Sunday harness which had grown hard and stiff from infrequent use and too small, having been made for her when she was younger. I also felt most uncomfortable in my good clothes, which were ever outgrown and held me like a corselet. At last the house door was locked and we drove the two miles to the church, silent and serious as became our Sunday clothes and our equipage. We felt strange to ourselves and not at ease. When the meeting was over I had a sudden overpowering revulsion in my spirits. I wanted to shout, to run, to jump over something and a hitching post as high as my head offered the nearest opportunity. I forgot the Sunday school lesson in a moment; I had not understood a word of it. On the way home we became very cheerful. There was comment on the wayside farms and gossip of the doings of the neighbors. We compared the height of their corn with our own field, and always found it a little less than ours. A heavy load of something seemed lifted from our hearts on returning from meeting. Uncle Lyman slyly put his quid back into his mouth which at once made him happier. There was a faint remonstrance from the back seat, which he pretended not to hear; or he would rejoin, "mother, have you munched all those caraway seeds you took along to meeting?" My driving on the way home was much like the illusion which follows us through life. Hands in front of ours direct our actions and our affairs. We hold but the slack of the reins, and the driven imagines himself the driver. There was a short whip in the socket, which was never taken out in the summer, and in sleighing disappeared altogether; it was only ornamental. "Hudup" and a flap of the reins were enough for the encouragement of Nancy. A switch of her tail and a laying back of her ears showed that she understood. If a letter must be written, it was done after meeting. Uncle Lyman seldom touched pen and paper except when an item was to be set down in his account book. Paper was scarce and costly and postage six good cents; and the pen, a quill, was usually dried up, and the nib opened too wide to hold the ink, and had to be soaked a good while before it would write. There was always some excuse for not answering a letter. But nothing pleased him more than to receive one. It was read slowly and with great attention, stuck behind the clock and reread for a week. The Sabbath ended with an early supper and early sleep, for Monday was always a busy day. Corn and potatoes did not rest on the Sabbath, neither did weeds.

At last for Uncle Lyman there came the eternal Sabbath day. He lifted the latch of his house door for the last time, smoked his last pipe, and laid down willingly to sleep. Other feet now traverse his lands; there is new paint over the ancient red house walls, and new labor saving tools; they and hired menials do the work, but no more than his two hands in proud industrious independence were wont to accomplish. He is forgotten by those who now possess what he made worth possessing. But I have not forgotten him, and little do the present owners of his houses and lands imagine that there is a title back of theirs, registered in the court of memory which no mere occupation and ownership can invalidate.

THE ANCIENT NEW ENGLAND FARMER

How pleasant o'er the still autumnal vale
 From his great timbered barn's wide open door
The muffled sound of his unresting flail
 In rhythmic swing upon the threshing floor!

How straight their tasselled tops his corn upreared!
 Straight were the rows, no weed dared raise its head;
How golden gleamed their opening sheaths well eared
 Whose inner husks stuffed out his bulging bed!

Full many a field of dewy grass breast-high
 His long sharp scythe ere breakfast time did lay;
Full many a hurrying shower came by,
 But to the mow still faster went the hay.

To him as inward fires were ice and snow,
 They urged his pulse with warm vivacious blood;
How made his furrowed cheeks in winter glow
 With ruddy health and iron hardihood!

Superfluous to him was coat or vest,
 Let blow hot or cold or stormiest weather;
He, as his hardy fathers, liked the best
 His shirt sleeves free and brimless cap of leather.

Few were his books, his learning was but small;
 He boasted not of thoughts beyond his speech;
Some few and simple maxims bounded all

That he had learned, or wished to teach.

He loved his home, his farm, his native town;
  These were the walls his happy world confined;
And heaven with unaccustomed joy looked down
  To see fulfilled a life itself designed.

Sadly his neighbors bore him to his grave
  Beneath the old perpetual mourning pine,
Where honest tears and praise they duly gave,
  For all he was, the immemorial sign.

THE DORR WAR AND MILLERISM

There was trouble enough in Bellingham in 1840. The sleepy old town in its previous existence had never felt a ripple of excitement more moving than a sewing bee, a travelling phrenologist or temperance lecturer, a summer picnic or a winter revival. Now it was invaded on one hand by Millerism and on the other by the Dorr War. The seat of the latter was in Rhode Island; but Bellingham, being a border town, was in danger of a raid. The Dorrites did, in fact, advance as far as Crook's Tavern on the southern boundary of the town, where, having drunk up what rum they could find, and hearing that the other tavern in the center of the town was kept on teetotal principles, they at once retreated. Not, however, before an alarm had been rung out by the church bell and the militia company called to arms. Great was the fright of the women and children. There was no sleeping in any house, no working and little eating for several days. My mother took her family to the top of a neighboring hill to reconnoitre and was prepared to run for the woods in case the enemy appeared. She was in great distress, having no man to care for and protect her little brood. She was a small, delicate and timid woman, extremely unfitted to play the heroine, and only used to suffering, which she bore like a saint. On the contrary I aged seven, armed with a long fishpole, threatened the advance of the rebels, and was eager to have them come on. I did not go far from my mother and sisters however. I enjoyed the situation, for I loved danger, with plenty of protection and means of escape. I loved fire, deep and threatening water, the roofs of houses, high, dangerous places, thin ice and a bull in the pasture. These tempted me to trials of boyish bravery. At heart, a little coward, I brandished my fishpole and clung to my mother's dress. We could see our soldiers with their high hats surmounted by pompons, parading in front of the town house and could hear the snare drum beat the time of their movement. Nothing came of the affair beyond great excitement and town talk. The Dorrites retreated to Smithfield, the militia men went back to their farms and the town was saved. I was terribly disappointed, and the succeeding days were too flat and dull to be endured. I got through them by playing at soldiering for the remainder of the summer, making forts and wooden guns and gay uniforms out of bright bits of calico, cocked hats of paper stuck full of cock tail feathers. I had also a long-handled lance which had come down in the family from Revolutionary times with which I charged the woodpile and the hen house, made of sods, at an angle in the orchard wall. Through this I thrust so fiercely one day that I killed our only rooster, to the consternation of my mother and sisters. As I was much in need of more tail feathers for my military hat, it did not seem to me such a tragedy. I was punished by not getting the drumstick and wishing bone when he was cooked, and the tail feathers, to my chagrin, were made into a hearth duster.

The Dorr Rebellion was not long past when the terrifying prophecies of Rev. William Miller began to be preached. He had figured out by Biblical and historical dates that the world was to last six thousand years, and that era would be reached about 1843. The Dorr scare was a trifle compared to the panic which now seized upon many people in the country towns of New England. Even those who disbelieved or scoffed could not conceal their dread. It sobered everybody and banished all joy and gaiety. A sad expectancy and presentiment of impending disaster oppressed whole communities. Church members and serious minded persons thought it as well to be prepared and to be on the safe side, in case the end should come. Revivals were going on everywhere and the churches were refilled. What impression did this talk and excitement make on children? I can say for one that I enjoyed it almost as much as the Dorr War. I comprehended nothing of what it meant. I never thought of anything happening to myself, to the house or my dog and kites. The general agitation filled me inwardly with a lively joy; the danger seemed to threaten only our neighbors, that is, such as were Millerites. I reasoned that they and their houses would somehow disappear while we should remain. So every morning I climbed a little hill to see if Sylvanus White's house was standing. He was the leading believer in the end of the world among our neighbors, a prosperous farmer living in a large, frame house. I heard my mother say that he had no children, and it did not make much difference to him what happened. I pondered this remark of my mother trying to think what she meant. I got no farther than the curious conclusion that all the Millerites were grown up people without children, and, by a natural deduction, that my mother and sisters and myself were safe from the end of the world. But I was not altogether satisfied. In my heart, so much did I delight in having something going on, that I wanted to see the great event, which I pictured to myself, remembering the words, flame, smoke and thunder, as something like the mimic Indian fights I had once seen represented on the annual training day of the militia men; only this promised to be on a grander scale.

It is well known that children play at death and funerals without sorrow; so I played the destruction of the world with great delight. I made my world of small boxes for houses, one over the other, and on top of all, a crippled kite which represented Farmer White, as I had heard that he had prepared a white robe in which to ascend. I wanted of course some people in my doomed world besides Farmer White. I manufactured quite an assemblage out of one thing and another and gave them names, mostly of older boys whom I disliked, my Sunday-school teacher, who gave me a bad half hour every week, and my uncle Slocomb who was always telling my mother I would never be a man if she did not stop indulging me so much. I added a few pretended animals of corn cobs, a dead snake, a live frog; and, as these did not seem the real thing, I tied my dog and cat and a lame chicken close to the sacrificial heap. I surrounded the whole with sticks, paper and pine cones and then came the exciting moment when I "touched her off," as boys say. What fun, what glee I experienced at that moment, no one can know, who does not keep in his bosom a fragment of his boyish heart. Creation may please the gods, but it cannot equal the boy's pleasure in destruction, especially by fire. I only needed a few spectators and I soon had them. The flames began to singe the dog and cat, and fricassee the chicken. Their howling and screaming brought the family upon the scene, and none too soon to save the lives of my pets. I was shut in a dark closet on bread and water for the remainder of the day and left to meditate, as my mother charged me, when I confessed my intentions, on "the naughtiness of mocking serious things." Thus did I innocently anticipate in my own person that *dies irae* which I had prepared for my imaginary town. I took no further interest in Millerism and in neighbor White's big house and ascension robe. After this I made new and less destructible worlds which continue to this day.

But the delusion did not expire by my neglect. It is still cherished as the candid faith of many readers of scriptural oracles. And now they are comforted by the astronomers who terrify us with their calculations on the inexorable cataclysm impending over our trusty and splendid earth. Never mind; we shall not be at the exit. To the vast future belong all these disconcerting predictions—and welcome. Time has already inscribed our urns, and, without mathematics, appointed for each one his separate and appropriate catastrophe. We who have lived fifteen lustrums have already witnessed the dissolution of our world. What more could the Rev. William Miller do for us?

WOODS AND PASTURES

There are many matters in the recollections of our earliest years so minute that to speak of them is only becoming to second childhood. "The soul discovers great things from casual circumstances", says Porphory. Providence provides temporary bridges through life which commonly fall to pieces after we pass over them and are forgotten. It is not so with me; one bridge remains whole and more beautified by time—that on which I return to my native town. I require no daylight or lantern for the journey. Some men can number their happy days; I more often count my happy nights, when I soothe myself to repose by recalling the sweet and tender joys of childhood. I travel the roads and pastures or wade the brook hand in hand with Launa Probana.

There was no gate out of Bellingham in my childhood. Its confines I never thought to question, or to suspect that there was anything beyond. It had its own sun, moon and stars, its river, its pond, its pastures and woods as full of interests and resources and as exhilarating as any place discovered later on the map of the world. This concentration and limitation give to children experiences and illusions which color the whole subsequent life. They are implicit in that soil where we find the roots of our being. They are what make us good citizens, steadfast friends, true lovers, observers of nature, disciples of the poets. They, whose early life is diffused over too many objects, with too many opportunities, have only a temporary and incomplete hold and delight in any of the advantages of their superior fortune. What is the good of however large a circle, if it have no center?

The lean and hungry pastures of Bellingham were prolific in inexhaustible harvests; what they bore on their surface may hint of something deeper and more perennial. The pastures and borders of the woods were covered with patches of huckleberry and blue-berry bushes, and over every stone heap clambered the low blackberry vines with racemes of luscious fruit. The pastures were named from one or the other of these berries, and their owners never claimed private right to them. To put up the bars as we entered and left the field, was the only obligation expected of us. Seldom were they taken down; the women crawled through, the boys leaped over, the small girls squeezed in between the posts and the wall. Our forefathers left the turnstile behind them in their English meadows, but not the short-cut from house to house, from field to field or from village to village. There is always a shorter way than the crowd travels. Boys and animals, those untaught explorers and surveyors, are the first to find it. Once within the pasture, a hundred short paths led hither and thither wherein grew a little low, sweet grass which the red cows grazed and sheep nibbled; and as they sauntered along they paid behind for their food in front. Then a warning voice would be raised telling us to be careful where we stepped. In these mazy pathways we were always returning upon our tracks and finding the bushes we had already stripped. Children were crying out to each other that the bottom of their pails was covered, or that they had a pint or quart, and generally as many went into the mouth as into the pail. The days when we went berrying were holidays, although the berries were picked for market and added a mite to the year's supply of silver money. Bank bills and gold we never saw, only silver and copper, and of these, silver was the money of men and women and huge copper cents and half cents of boys. I can remember a time when one cent was riches unspeakable, treasured for months and often displayed in triumph to penniless companions. Poor indeed are they who have never known the day of small things and the size of a cent. It is said money is only good for what it will buy, and the miser who hoards is the scoff of mankind. I must have been a descendant of Shylock for I loved cents for themselves and the feeling of importance they gave me. I polished them until they shone like gold and the face of the Father of his Country gleamed with irridescent benignity. Some were hopelessly worn and battered; some had a hole in them or a piece nicked out of the rim. These I exchanged with my mother for more perfect ones which I could burnish.

For children, berrying was play, pure pastime; it brought no money to their pockets. For the first hour it was infinitely exciting; by the next, we wanted something else, and it was difficult to keep us in order. What to do next is an eternal question that has followed both children and man from Eden. It is usually resolved by doing the same thing over again.

A little boy once sat discontentedly on the bank of a river. A traveller asked him what was the matter. He answered "I want to be on the other side of the stream." "What for?" inquired the traveller. "So that I could come back here," said the restless boy.

To hide and play games was one means of escape from the fatigue of the slow filling berry pails. Then such quiet fell over the pasture that our elders knew some mischief was afoot. We were promptly discovered, scolded and warned that we must fill our pails before we could play.

As milking time approached we gathered up stray hats, aprons and handkerchiefs and prepared to go home. We painted each others' cheeks with the red blood of huckleberries and crowned our heads with leaves of the birch and oak, stalks of indigo weed or broad fern fronds that hung down over the face like green veils. Thus freaked and marked, walking in single file, our mothers and elder sisters behind us, shouting, leaping and laughing, we presented something as near a Bacchic procession as could be found in a community enshrouded in the black cloak of John Calvin. What a good time it was to be alive, and never is a boy so young as in the berry pasture, nor any place so full of enchantments. She—for it was never a boy—who had picked the most berries that day, headed the band and was a proud and envied person. Our elders cherished this emulation. I was always thinking that the next time we went berrying, I should try for the head of the procession; but the fun was too much for me; I could not hold to my resolution above a half hour; I was excessively fond of praise but averse to the ways of meriting it. The only long word I brought away from childhood was approbativeness. I never used the word, nor knew its meaning, and, least of all, could have pronounced it. I heard it once only, together with another word, editor, which I understood as little, from the lips of a travelling phrenologist. It happened that my mother lodged and fed him for a night and he paid his score by examining the heads of all the family. I was greatly impressed when he remarked that I had a large bump of approbativeness and would sometime be an editor. As to the bump, feeling over my own head, I never could find it. My mother said it was inside and that the phrenologist meant I must be a good boy. I was quite used to that interpretation of everything concerning myself. A great many years after, when I became editor of an obscure newspaper, so little comfort, reputation or profit did I find in it, that I amused myself in thinking of it as the fulfillment of the phrenologist's prophecy.

The Bacchic procession dropped its members here and there along the road and we got to our own cottage tired, sunburnt and hungry. We ate our suppers of berries and milk out of pewter porringers with pewter spoons and went to bed at dark. The next day we fed on berry pies, and all the neighborhood during the berry season bore the marks of pies in blackened teeth and lips, except a few fastidious young women who cleaned theirs with vinegar. Tooth brushes were as unknown as rouge and powder. Every Saturday night the children were scrubbed in a wash tub in front of the fire place in winter, and at the door in summer. During the session of school my mother washed my ears and face every day, pinned my collar, kissed me, and always her tedious parting injunction was, mind your teacher, study your lesson and be a good boy. Then away with flying feet I overtake my companions, whom no sooner met, than we loitered along the road, hand in hand, or arms around another's neck, merry and playful, quite unmindful of nine o'clock and the hateful lesson. There were no precocious and wonderful children in our red school house. Even I did not begin to write poetry until I was eighteen or nineteen! The only literary prodigy among our neighbors was a maiden lady who wrote obituary verses on the death of her pious friends.

The berry season lasted several weeks, and toward its close prudent housewives dried some for winter use or preserved them in molasses. The last we gathered were the swamp, or high-bush blueberries. These had a sub-acid, delicious flavor, not unlike the smell of the swamp pink, which grew in the same spot. The black raspberry, which we called thimble berry, was found along the stone walls, but was not abundant. I knew a few bushes and kept it secret, for if I found a saucerful I was sure of a small pie baked by my mother, and all my own. If I could not find enough for a pie I strung such as I gathered on long spears of grass. As they were shaped like little thimbles, I fitted them on the grass stems one over the other like a nest of cups, reversing them at intervals, to make a pattern, which showed the young savage, generally intent only on something to eat or to play with, to have a slight artistic instinct. As I now recall those strings of thimble berries, I think they would make an humble ornamental border to a picture of a New England roadside with its crooked and tumbled stone walls. No road to me is attractive that is not bounded by such walls and fringed with berry bushes, brush and wild apple trees, from among which peer forth the cymes of the wayfaring bush and sweet scented clusters of the traveller's joy. Let England have her trim, hawthorne lanes and pleached gardens of fruit and flower, and Italy her olive and orange; for me the New England wilding roadside, interrupted only now and then by a farmhouse and littered yard, is dearer.

I have not yet mentioned other berries that used to make a country boy's life so full of interest. There was the cranberry, not yet exploited by cultivation and proprietorship. In Bellingham the cranberry meadows were still wild and free. The farmer who claimed an exclusive right to them had no standing in the community and was universally denounced as mean and stingy. No one wanted many, as they were not bought at country stores, and, required as much sugar in the cooking as there were berries; so cranberry sauce was a luxury rarely indulged. Like most wild fruits they were never picked clean. When the spring thaws flooded the meadows and washed them in windrows on the shore we gathered them to eat raw and also for paint. Having been frozen and a little sweetened in their winter and watery wanderings, we found them more palatable than when cooked. I know not why, yet a country boy prefers the raw and wild flavor far more than the condiments and seasonings of cookery. The chief use of the spring cranberries was as a paint; the thin juice made a pretty, pink color on white paper, or added an admirable touch to a russet, red cheek, such as commonly beautified Bellingham boys and girls, nurtured on milk, apples and brown bread, open air and unfinished attic chambers.

I dwell much on the recollections of the doings of the day, but the nights had also their joys, none greater than the rain on the roof and the exquisite, semi-conscious moments when sleep began to overtake body and soul, gently extinguishing them in a soothing, delicious languor. The low country attic is the true house of dreams, where the good, the strange or the fearful spirits play over the subjected and helpless will. Long time I remembered some of those dreams which visited my truckle bed, placed on rollers a foot from the floor and thrice as many from the ridge pole. In winter, tightly tucked in by a loving mother, the cold without only made me feel the more snug and warm within. The snow sifted through the chinks in the loose shingles, making little white hillocks on the floor, and often I found enough on my pillow in the morning to press into a snowball and pelt my sister, who slept at the other end of the attic.

I follow no order in my narrative: I wander; but how can one go far in the small and circumscribed region of earliest memories, bound each to each by some inwardly felt affinity, which neither time nor world wanderings can dissever? One thing suggests another and the connection must be found in the things themselves. Cranberry picking carried me forward into springtime; now I return to the autumn, the harvest season, when although not old enough to dig my mother's small patch of potatoes, I could pick them up in a basket. She herself handled the hoe uncovering the long reds and the white Chenangos. I liked better to shake down apples than to gather things from the ground; for to climb trees is as much a boy's as a monkey's instinct. That was my first thought when I happened to observe any kind of tree, could I climb it? The wild grapes which grew in profusion along the banks of our river clambering over the tall grey birches gave me glorious opportunities for climbing, as the sweetest and largest clusters were always at the very top of the trees. The limbs of the grey birch, although small, are very elastic and tough, making a sure footing for the climber. The danger was, that, as he approached the slender spire of the tree, it would suddenly bend or break and drop him into the water. This was all the more fun, if he could swim. When he reached home he was liable to have his jacket not only dried but "warmed," which was the colloquial for a thrashing. I usually sold grapes enough during the day of the Fall militia training to keep me in pocket money through the winter. This was my first effort at any kind of trading and, I think, spoilt me for a commercial career; for there was no cost, no capital, no loss; all was profit; and ever since that day it has seemed to me the only manner of doing business worth while. There are, or were, other compensations in a life of trade, which might fire the ambition of a strenuous youth. I remember three voyages made the merchant a Thane in ancient England.

When frost began to brown the grass and brighten the trees, the woods were full of boys, partridges and squirrels. The boys and squirrels, much alike in their appetites and ability to climb trees, were intent on gathering a store of nuts for winter. In early morning after a sharp frost, the chestnut burrs opened and the nuts dropped out, falling and hiding among the leaves. There we hunted for them; the squirrels did not appear to have to hunt, but put their intelligent paws under the leaves with an infallible instinct. They were always on the ground earlier than we, and filled their cheeks before we had filled our bags and pockets. What extraordinary care the chestnut takes of herself; a rough outer garment bristling with sharp needles, and within, the whitest, silkiest lining fit for the cradle of a baby queen. To prevent accidents and a more easy delivery from the burr, the nut is annointed with a slight exudation of oil, which gives a soft, agreeable feeling as you hold it in your hand. Doubtless it acts as a preservative also keeping the nut from becoming too soon dry and hard. Chestnuts were laid away for future use, to be brought out on winter evenings with cider and apples. Nobody thought of going to bed without first eating something. Sometimes the chestnuts were roasted in the ashes on the hearth, and less often boiled. Of all places to warm them, a boy's pocket was the best; there they were handiest to eat on the road, or at school, when the teacher was not looking. If caught in the act, you were called up to her desk and forfeited the contents of your pocket. It might be returned to you if you had behaved yourself meanwhile and had not whispered, thrown spit balls, or pinched the little girl who sat next to you. There were two kinds of walnut trees in the neighborhood; the common name of one was shagbark, of the other pignut. The shagbark was the walnut of the market, a nut with a rich, oily kernel; the pignut was smaller with a very thick shell and correspondingly small meat, hard to separate from the shell. They were of little worth, not salable and we gathered them only when the other kind was scarce. It took a hard frost, several times repeated, to loosen them from the tree. We often clubbed them down. It was a perilous undertaking to climb a walnut tree, for the limbs began to grow high up and the trunk was covered with a rough bark, hence the name shagbark; to shin up, and still more to descend, was apt to make patches or a new seat to your trousers your mother's evening work after you had gone to bed. Where grew anything good to eat and free to all, a boy was sure to have it, although it cost him subsequent patches, whippings and tears. Shall the squirrel hunt for nuts and the little sons of men be forbidden, just to save a new pair of breeches, or an old jacket? But the woes of country boyhood are naught in comparison to its joys, and a day in a berry field, or a morning among the chestnut trees, under the blue sky and a west wind, with merry companions, is a memory that outshines all the purchased pleasures of later life. Confess to me, ye humble and trivial things, confess what charms were yours, which never the flood of years submerges. Alas, they have no speech. I hear but a strain of imperishable music.

APPRENTICESHIPS

HOME AND HOMESICKNESS

It was thought best in New England country towns that boys, who were not needed on the farm and were not to be educated beyond the common school, should learn some trade. As my mother possessed no land nor any means to send me to academy and college, it was early decided to apprentice me to a trade with some good master. There was another reason; she did not feel able nor competent to manage me when I should be older. She had a presentiment that it would require a stronger hand than her own gentle one to guide me in a straight path. Always after the death of her husband, her only means of meeting her difficulties and perplexities was by prayer. Three times each day, after the morning, noon and evening meals she retired to her own chamber to pray. She read none but religious books and the Bible. Her Bible was the wedding gift of her husband—that and one silver spoon marked with his and her initials J. A. and E. T. intertwined after the manner of silversmiths. My father appears to have been the owner of but one book, Cotton Mather's, "Essays to do Good," which I still possess and, alas, could never read through. Of course the title of the volume at the date of its republication, 1808, had been greatly reduced. No Mather would be satisfied with a title much less expansive than the contents, nor wanting some Latin interlardings. The original title was "Benifacias," followed by ten lines of sub-titles. This was unusual reserve for one of Cotton Mather's productions. In its day it was as popular as is the worst novel of ours, and was continually being republished. Even Dr. Franklin read and praised it and professed that it had influenced his whole life. The preface is a fine specimen of the manner in which a popular Boston preacher at the beginning of the eighteenth century expressed himself when he appeared in print. It has all the airs and attudinizing of a full dress ball-room. He says that a passage in the speech of a British envoy suggested the book and declares of it, "Ink were too vile a liquor to write that passage. Letters of gold were too mean to be the preservers of it. Paper of Amyanthus would not be precious and perennous enough to perpetuate it."

A prayerful mother, the Bible and the Rev. Cotton Mather ought to have been sufficient to turn out good boys from any household. Then there was Sunday-school where we were much instructed about the nature and consequences of sin and the end that awaited bad boys. Notwithstanding, some closer and more practical guidance was needed for a growing lad; something to put him in the way of preparing to earn his living. Accordingly in my eighth year I was turned over to an uncle, my father's only brother, who lived in the next town. He was a boot maker with four sons of his own. At once I found myself cut off from all the objects and persons I had ever known, thrown into a strange world, my own lost as completely as if I had gone to another. I found myself introduced to a small room up a flight of stairs at the end of the shed of my uncle's house. The room was full of windows, all of which looked in the direction of my lost home; it had a number of low shoemaker's benches ranged along three of its sides. Here my uncle and two of his sons made boots. I was directed to one of the benches and began by being taught how to use a waxed end and stitch the counters of bootlegs. Never in my life before had I been pinned to one spot for any length of time save on a school bench; never before set at any work that was not or that could not be made half play. A deadly home-sickness at once seized upon me, of which I could not be cured by all the kindness and encouragement of my uncle and aunt. I was constantly looking out of the shop windows, expecting some one to come and rescue me. Constantly I wept and could not swallow my food for the lump in my throat; at last food was loathsome and my eyes became so swollen with continual tears that I could scarcely see to thread my needle. Thus I suffered for three weeks and my young heart was wounded and broken past all cure. My nature was changed from that time; a kind of depression and melancholy, took the place of my natural gaiety. I can readily believe, such were my misery and agony, that one might die of home-sickness. I recall it so well that I can diagnose its symptoms which are like those of a fever. It comes over one in paroxysms, followed by a great calm as from sudden cessation of acute pain, then by a choking sensation, a terrible sinking of the heart, down, down, all things swim in the convulsion of lost senses until tears once more relieve the overwrought soul. To add to my misery my two young cousins would have nothing to do with me. For the entire three weeks I never spoke a word; the moment I tried I choked and burst into tears. No wonder my cousins and other boys avoided me. Such a baby was past their comprehension or tolerance. In my own natural place I should have had no more mercy on such an one. It is remarkable how early boys begin to trim each other into manly character; they instantly discover and attack any little weakness, and with rough and ready hand or tongue make the weakling or the upstart ashamed of himself. But no treatment harsh or kind could cure a homesick child, and one day my uncle said he was going to see my mother, and that I was to go with him. Oh, how my spirits recovered themselves! I never thought of the return; only to go, to be once more in my own home, with my own river, fields and companions, filled me with ecstacy. I went and I did not return. I did not know what was said between my mother and uncle; I saw him drive away and leave me behind with unspeakable joy. For many subsequent days I observed my mother's sorrowful eyes when she spoke to me. Her first experiment, which promised so well, had failed. If she was disappointed, I was sobered and much easier to manage from that time forth: I tried to please my mother. Our old way of life went on its usual round. Again the little Red House was happy. I resumed my play under the garden apple tree or on the great rock in the corner of the orchard. That year I mastered the alphabet, and I was given a slate and pencil for the purpose of keeping me still when not saying my letters. The school days of that period are memorable to me, chiefly from the recesses and the noon intermission an hour long. It was in that hour I became intimate with some little girls, and found that I liked them as well as boy playmates. How we choose our favorite companions, no man is wise enough to know; yet choice there certainly was, with no formality or effort. How could it be otherwise? From the troop by the door or the roadside, eating their dinner from basket or pail or playing games, some predestined affinity drew away a boy and maid to the birchen bower, where with one mind they set up mimic housekeeping and forbade the entrance of strange children. There one cloak covered them both. Or they rambled hand in hand through the woods, or waded in the shallow water of Beaver brook down to the stone arch bridge where the confined streamlet gurgled softly over the slimy pebbles, and the arch echoed to the sound of their voices. What matter though pantalets and little breeches, pulled up as high as they could be, were wet with jumping and splashing; hot sun and warm blood would soon dry them. Wrinkles and limpness might betray them when they returned to the mother's fold at night, but her reproaches had no terror nor any restraint for happy children, who alone know the secrets of their own pleasures and have no remembrance of interference with them. With boy and boy there is a perfect equality; no pretentions are allowed, except those of age. With maid and boy it is different. With my companion, I wished to appear superior, to show her things, even to attempt to explain them; and thus I myself learned to observe natural objects and to love them. She was my teacher, although I believed myself hers. She listened, she looked up at me and asked another question, and so I see her to this day. How should I not become wise? If not, it is no fault of hers. My Launa, whom I led through the woods, along the water courses, and to whom I promised, that some day we would catch a cloud and ride around the sky visiting the moon and stars, yes, it was Launa to whom I promised everything, and promised because she wished it, and I felt it my business to seem able to gratify all her desires. She already led me captive; well she knew it, and loved to test me with impossible demands. She dared me to do a hundred things, which attempting and failing, I boldly declared I had done. Just as willing to be deceived as I to deceive, she never questioned my lie, but led me on to some fresh feat, some brook or fence to leap, or inaccessible flower or berry to bring her. Already I got out of difficulties by changing the subject, by evading the challenge and diverting her to some other object, play or plan to which she as readily listened. How proud, how important and superior I felt and with what trust the little siren permitted it. Among all my apprenticeships this to Launa Probana was that which taught me most and is most ineffaceable.

THE SAW-MILL

The next effort to make a craftsman of me was in my tenth year. I was put under the hands of a mill-wright. He set up the machinery of saw and grist mills and repaired them when out of order. He had a saw mill and shingle mill of his own, but he was often away from home, especially in winter, and then I ran the saw mill alone. Its machinery was old fashioned and now obsolete, an upright saw, a carriage for the logs somewhat like that now in use, but much heavier and more clumsy. To set the logs to the required width of boards or other lumber we used inch rules, a bar made on purpose for the work and dogs to hold the logs in place. The power was water turned upon the floats of a large wheel. No large timber was left in the neighborhood, otherwise a boy of ten could not have run the mill alone; but with a cant-hook I could usually manage to roll the log upon the carriage and put it in position. We ran off the slabs first and these were the perquisites of the mill owner. They were used in his own family and some were sold or given to poor widows and others. The saw mill was run only in winter time; the water of the mill pond was drawn off in early spring, and where it had flooded the land, grass grew in summer. While the log was running through the saw, it was my never ending delight to lean out of an opening in the side of the mill and watch the tailrace rush from under the building. All winter I looked forward to the day when the great gates of the dam would be raised and the pond disappear in a few hours. I cannot exactly describe the feeling with which, after a few days of sunshine. I walked over the ground where the water had stood; a strange commingling of awe and curiosity, especially as I threaded the now dry, narrow and deep canal, which led the water of the pond to the mill. There I often walked just to enjoy in imagination the thought, what if the water should suddenly come pouring down upon me! I even selected the best places to escape up the rough stone walls of the canal. All my boyhood I enjoyed thrilling imaginary perils, and the planning means of escape. The walls of this canal were made of irregular stones from the field. Alternately wet and dry they had taken on beautiful colors, variegated according to the character of the stone, and between them in summer, and quite covering them in places, grew many kinds of wild flowers, mosses and ferns, and, most splendid of all, the cardinal flower. The canal was always damp, and a few frogs and green snakes made it their summer home. Do not imagine I made any such observations as these at the time, least of all that I then knew the cardinal flower by its correct name. I saw, I felt, I dreamed; now I remember and know a little more. I lacked the right name and reason for most things, but knowing nothing, I named everything after my own fancy and found the creation as good and sweet as the Creator at the end of his week's work. Every boy is a new Adam, and christens the world of his senses in the most primitive figure of language, metonomy.

The terms of my apprenticeship included a new suit of clothes each year, and that I should be sent to school in the summer. The clothes were never forthcoming and my mother had to furnish them. My master gave me my boots for winter and shoes for summer, but I went barefooted seven months of the year. This was no hardship. How I hated to wear shoes on the only day when it was compulsory, Sunday. It cost me tears to learn to tie a double bow knot with my shoestring, as my master insisted upon my doing, and this was the only thing during my apprenticeship that he took pains to teach me—to tie a shoestring. He was a silent, self-absorbed man with a stern manner, a square set jaw, wide mouth and ponderous ears. He was very fond of his two little girls, three and four years old; but he never had a kind word for me. However, he was not peculiar in this respect. Boys were not cosseted in those days, but made to feel the rod and keep their place. It seems to me now that I must have been to him a necessary nuisance, tolerated for what service I could render, yet I was not unhappy. My mother lived across the road and I could see her every day. I had some time for play; the mills, the tools, the dam and canals interested me and beyond all, I fished to my heart's content. There was an old mongrel dog at my heels wherever I went, and together we hunted woodchucks and squirrels without a gun. In the evening, by the stove, he still hunted them in his dreams, whimpering and barking as soon as he was sound asleep, and I myself often had the same dream when I had been unusually excited by the sport. In the autumn I set snares for partridges which I sold to the Boston stage drivers for nine-pence apiece. Well do I remember the high hope with which I entered the silent wood in early morning to examine my snares, the exhilaration when I found a poor partridge in the noose, limp and dead, with a white film drawn over her eyes. Pity for bird or beast or human beings was an unknown feeling then: I liked to torment such life as I had power over, to see it suffer. The sale of partridges furnished me with considerable spending money; for what I spent it, I know not. I am only certain I did not hoard it, as I have never found any ancient silver pieces in my purse or pockets. I can think of no more entertaining account book than one which should show the acquisition and outlay of a boy's money; his financial statement from his fifth to his fifteenth year. I should like to audit such an account and, however, it came out I would agree to find it correctly cast, balanced and properly vouched; for a boy always gets his money's worth and thinks he has what he wants. In his trades with other boys, money seldom plays any part, and the little swindler always believes he has got the best of the bargain. And why? Because he has what he coveted, and what was another's. Somehow the other fellow's knife is a little better than his own, it is three blades to his two. When he finds the cheat he has only to swap again. In this way I traded a dozen times in one summer and came out with one blade, but a bright brass haft.

By this time I could read and even imitate the copies set in the writing books. This, however, was not the real method by which I had learned to use the pen or rather pencil. Much more skill was acquired in little notes to Launa Probana during school hours, passed furtively under the desks and benches or hidden in a book which I was suddenly anxious to borrow or lend. What nothings we wrote! With what pains and searchings of the brain for words! Still I filled my bit of paper while Launa wrote only three words, yet her name signed in the tiniest letters satisfied me. With that name in my vest pocket I felt her near me, fixed my attention upon my book again, and learned my lessons more easily. I was conscious that she watched all my movements out of the corner of her eye, and at recitations it was she, who, when I hesitated and was lost, bending her head down so as not to be observed by the teacher, whispered softly the right word and saved me from shame. Thus in a thousand ways she repaid the boy's devotion, and however out-spelt or out-grammared he might be, where he stood, was for her the head of the class. What lessons we learned, not in any book nor taught by any teacher! After a year or two more of winter saw-mill and summer school my teacher thought I was old enough to write compositions, an exercise usual in all New England common schools. Long before this I thought myself competent and was ambitious to begin. It seemed too much a school exercise to be undertaken out of it. I saw the older pupils on appointed afternoons stand up in their places and read from their slates the compositions they had written. It fired my ambition beyond any of the other exercises or lessons. It seemed to me the very pinnacle of greatness to stand up and read a composition before the whole school. How I labored over my first little essay, not being able to think of anything, or to find language; how I began without any real beginning sentences that had no end; how I strung together words without connection or sense, how the whole school tittered and made faces as I read, how I sat down flushed, trembling, completely overwhelmed with mortification, it pains me even to remember. What would Launa care for me now! Without seeming to notice her I looked over to where she sat and saw that she was weeping. I did not speak to her for a whole week. Thus I punished myself, and all the week pondered how I could write something which should make her again proud of me and reinstate myself with my teacher and schoolmates. Suddenly it occurred to me that next time I would choose a subject of which I knew something. Wonderful discovery, which has been of use to me ever since; a bit as well as reins—this is the reason why I have not been a prolific writer. Between one book and the next I am totally forgotten. I found also thus early that one needs a muse. I had made a blunder in not taking Launa into my counsels, say rather into my mind, for I had never once thought of her while writing, nor that she would be my audience. No, I thought only of myself, and the distinction I should win all for myself. Thus experienced, I did not repeat my mistake. When we were next called upon for compositions, I coaxed Launa to go with me at the nooning to the shade of the old blacksmith shop, where I proposed that we should write them together. There sentence by sentence I made my little essay, covering one side of my slate, with Launa for inspirer and critic. My subject was the saw-mill, that one I knew best. There was a pricking of ears in the school-room when I named my humble subject, and an elder boy by my side whispered, "Now, give us some sawdust." I prospered this time and won a smile from Launa. Had I helped her at all in her own composition? I know not; yet when she read, it seemed to me I had written it myself. Such has always been my experience in regard to writing which I have admired, and thought I could do as well—until I tried.

Thus passed two happy summers and two lonely impatient winters; then I was ill with a fever and came to the doors of death. I never resumed my apprenticeship to the mill-wright. For some years succeeding my illness I suffered from periodical sick headache which, before and after, was accompanied by a dreadful depression, an indescribable apathy, a distaste for food, for play, for everything: I wished myself dead. My mother and sisters were very tender to me at this time; they amused me, they petted me, and in the evening read to me stories out of Merry's Museum and from the school readers. It was at this time I was sent on a visit to Boston, perhaps for my health and spirits. I say sent, for I went alone in a stage coach the thirty miles. Much preparation was made for my journey and many letters passed to relatives in Boston concerning it. I had a new cloak lined with bright red flannel, home-made, and a cap with an extremely flat crown and a tassel that fell upon my shoulder. These were the first articles of clothing that made me feel that everybody was looking at me, a feeling something between vanity and embarrassment. My cousin met me in Boston at the stage office and took me to his house in the old West End, at that time the residence of the respectable middle class, with here and there some more wealthy citizens. There were a few shops at the corners of the streets; but I did not venture beyond the street where my cousin lived and saw nothing at all of the city. I was taken to church on Sunday and once to the Museum, where I saw the elder Booth in Shylock. The only scene that made an impression upon me was that where Shylock is about to take his pound of flesh. He squatted upon the floor, his wild and terrible face turned directly upon me, as it seemed, while he sharpened his knife upon his rusty shoe. I was filled with terror and began to cry and begged to be taken away. Quite angry, yet pitying me, too, I suppose, my cousin led me out and home where I went at once to bed, covering my head tightly, unable to sleep for apprehension lest I should be discovered by Shylock. At the Players' Club, in New York City, in the last winter of Edwin Booth's life, I related this incident to him as a childish tribute to his father's power. "Yes," he said, "that was my father, and such things often happened among women and children when he was playing that character. He was dangerous at times, not to his audiences, but occasionally to his fellow actors."

I returned from Boston not much wiser nor more travelled than when I went. I found nothing there that gave me so much pleasure as the freedom of my own field, my sports and my companions. When asked what I had seen, what I had done, I candidly confessed, nothing; yet among boys I did feel a certain pride because I was the only one among them who had been to Boston. And I have found the result of nearly all travel is little more than the cheap avenue to conversation between those who have travelled over the same ground, or the feeling of superiority that one has wandered farther.

Although I was more active and restless than most boys, ever longing, yet with no definite object, I believe I should always have remained in the place of my birth, except for family exigencies, for I had no ambitions, no special talent nor practical faculty. When I reflect on the futility of literature without genius, or the miserly rewards of scholarship, or the disastrous conclusion in a majority of business enterprises, I confess the life of a New England farmer is to be preferred. It was so ordered that opportunities, which I never could have made for myself, came to me unsought and without effort. Such education as I have, a miscellany of odds and ends of learning, and such things as I have accomplished, are the chance results of various and disconnected impulses; and God himself has given me my beautiful friends. I have found them waiting for me all along my path, and their attachment has always filled me with astonishment and gratitude; for I cannot think it is anything I have done that should deserve it. So I relegate it to that indefinable, unconscious self which is hidden from our own knowledge. On the whole, who is he, that would not rather be loved for himself than for his book, his horses or his honors? He, who is capable of friendship, and inspires it, is happier than Alexander with worlds conquered and to be conquered.

After much counselling and agitating of the change, my mother moved from Bellingham, which was her native place, to Hopkinton; and, from this time forth to the end of her life, she continued to change her residence from town to town as work, cheaper rent, or the persuasion of friends induced her. My eldest sister and I went with her. The change filled me with a pleasant excitement although we were going to the same place and the very same house where I had suffered so much from home-sickness. I did not then know that in leaving my birthplace I left behind me the fountain head of half my later musings, regrets and imaginings. In returning now, I find naught but the graves of my family, the elm of my childhood, fallen to the ground, its bleached trunk and larger limbs reminding me of a skeleton, the well filled with stones, and the Red House converted into a woodshed. The river still flows by; one great pine still murmurs and wonders what has become of the children once playing in its shade; the pond, the arched bridge which spanned its outflow are unchanged. And Launa, I fear to inquire what has become of her, though I never lost her. She followed and reappeared in all my wanderings.

BOOTMAKING

In Hopkinton I began to feel myself too old to play with girls. Boys were numerous and knew more than those I had met before. I soon caught up with their manners and customs, and in some respects bettered them. I outdid them in mischief, looted the best apple trees, beat them at ball and managed to escape my tasks oftener. My work was stitching the counters of boots; my mother and sister filled their spare time with the same employment. Indeed, at this period it was our sole means of support. The making of boots, pegged boots, double soled and welted, with legs treed until they were as stiff and hard as boards, was the chief occupation of all that portion of the town called Hayden Row. For a mile or more up and down this street were the houses of the bootmakers, each with its little shop, either attached to the house, or built in the yard. Each had from two to six workers. Generally every part of the boot was made in these shops; the stock was cut and distributed from some larger shop to which the finished boots were returned to be put in cases and shipped. The smaller shops were the centers for the gossip, rumors and discussions which agitated the community. There men sharpened their wits upon each other, played practical jokes, sang, argued the questions of that day, especially slavery, and arranged every week from early spring to late autumn a match game of ball either among themselves or the bootmakers of neighboring towns for Saturday afternoon, which was their half holiday. All this was possible where the men sat on low benches, making scarcely any noise, and doing work which did not often require concentrated attention. My uncle was a stern abolitionist, as were the other bootmakers; and before I knew it, I was one; nor did I know at that time that there was any other opinion in the world. Little did I understand or care for the subject. My uncle took the Liberator, and it was sometimes read aloud in the shop, and I can remember feeling angry at some of the stories of cruelty to slaves. I am glad I was brought up in such an atmosphere, for I have not changed on this point, as I have in so many other of my beliefs. The only church in the place was the Methodist, and my mother had, almost for the first time since her conversion at the age of fourteen, an opportunity of mingling with the brethren and sisters of her own faith. The chief financial pillar of the Methodists of New England, Lee Claflin, was a citizen of Hopkinton, although his place of business was Boston. He was, when I knew him, a rather short, fat man with a large head and a face beaming with benevolence and good will. To be noticed, to be spoken to by him was a great honor, so that when he laid his hand upon my head and inquired if I were a child of grace, although I had not the least idea what he meant, I was equal to the occasion and said, "Yes, sir." My mother smiled at my confession and I have no doubt her heart was made glad; for though she was not at all rigid in the religious discipline of her children, the great desire of her life was that they should be converted and saved from the toils of Satan. I had, as early as I had any conception of my own, a certain image of Satan as something huge, an aggregation of all the largest objects with which I was most familiar, arms and legs as long as the tallest trees and church steeples, and it was of his size that I was afraid, rather than of his temptations and torments, which I heard thundered from the pulpit. I had a fear, born of sundry rough encounters with larger boys, of that which was superior in strength, and to me Satan was as a big and ugly boy, whom I sometimes looked for along the road, expecting him to dart out from behind the stone walls, or clumps of bushes. Many writers have said harsh things about the former religious creeds and preaching of our New England forefathers, especially in their effects upon children. I do not agree with them. It did often save the wayward from peril, and offered a rich field for the imaginative interpretations of children. What does the modern child find in a modern sermon to give him any sort of quickening? Yes, my dear pulpit orators, with no wing left to imp your eloquence, recover Satan in all his immense, Miltonic grandeur and energy.

Those happy Hopkinton days were filled with many new and fascinating objects and boyish pursuits to which I gave an undivided heart. I learned all the tricks and sleight-of-hand with which the bootmakers amused themselves and puzzled each other in their shops. I was long in discovering the secret of the best trick of all, which was making names and pictures appear on the bare plaster of the shop walls by striking on them with a woolen cap such as we all wore. Then there were all sorts of string, button and ball tricks, and my pockets were full of articles with which to astonish the uninitiated. He, who introduced or invented a new trick or puzzle, was the hero of the shops for a day; and for many days after, as soon as learned, the men and boys were confounding each other by its performance. In those days Signor Blitz was travelling the country, giving his necromantic shows, and left behind him everywhere a taste for his wonderful performances. Our ingenuity was exercised in weaving watch chains in various patterns with silk twist; in making handsome bats for ball, and in making the balls themselves with the ravelled yarn of old stockings, winding it over a bit of rubber, and in sewing on a cover of fine thin calf skin. This ball did not kill as it struck one, and, instead of being thrown to the man on the base, was more usually thrown at the man running between them. He who could make a good shot of that kind was much applauded, and he who was hit was laughed at and felt very sheepish. That was true sport, plenty of fun and excitement, yet not too serious and severe. The issue of the game was talked over for a week. I did my daily stint of stitching with only one thing in mind, to play ball when through; for the boys played every afternoon. When there was to be an important match game the men practised after the day's work was done.

Meanwhile my education was entirely neglected. I attended no school at this time, either summer or winter, and came as near acquiring a trade as I have ever done. In fact I longed to be able to make the whole of a boot, to last, peg, trim, gum, blackball and stone it, all processes of the craft as then practised. But how does one know when he is learning? I was laying up a good store of things more valuable than any in books, whilst the free life I led was preparing in me the soft and impressionable tablets on which could be traced future experiences and acquisitions of a more intellectual kind. Tomorrow would come and this was its preparation. Yet not consciously can one prepare for it all that it is to hold. I became a graduate of the shops of the bootmakers before acquiring the whole of their trade, but not before absorbing most of that which constituted the overflow of their lives. I began to imitate the manners and conversation of men. Ridiculed for this, I retreated into myself and became more observant and more silent. A small, very dim yet new light appeared to me—reflection, silent thoughts at night, and when alone; questionings with no least effort at answers. My new world as yet was not much more than a mile square, as in my native town; within that mile I knew every natural object and all the people. Everybody called me by my first name, prefixing, usually, "little curly" or "snub-nose," and my companions gave me nicknames according to their likes or dislikes. I much affected the company of boys older than myself, especially my cousins, whom I naturally looked up to and very much admired. They would have none of me, called me "nuisance" and "tag-tail." This last epithet wounded me sorely and made me slink away like a whipped cur. Added to my mile-square world, I had now also the germs of memory. Faintly and at long intervals I remembered my life in Bellingham; but it seemed another planet, far off, indistinct, and I had as yet no desire to return to it.

LOVE AND LUXURY

My mother had three daughters, one had died within a year of my father's death. She was the belle of the neighborhood, fair-haired and blue-eyed, not very tall, graceful and attractive. Every one admired her and her friends loved her ardently. She had already ventured into verse, religious in tone, and affectionate effusions to her girl friends. With a little education she had begun to teach school. She was my first teacher and the school her first. We were very fond of each other. Her kiss was the only one I did not shrink from and try to escape. She took most of the care of me, and I always slept in the same room with her. Usually I went to sleep in her bed, and in the morning crept back into it. When death came and took her away from me, when I found, in the darkened room to which my mother led me where she lay in a white dress, that she did not kiss me nor even speak, I was frightened and awed. In a short time I forgot her; but before I grew to be a man I recovered her, and shed the tears long due her love and loss. Another older sister was already a successful teacher in the district schools of the region, so successful indeed, that she taught winters as well as summers, which was unusual for women teachers to attempt. Several winters she had undertaken schools, the pupils of which were so unruly that no man could be found who was able to control them. At length, through friends who knew her success and abilities, she was invited to take charge of a private school in Norwich, Connecticut. Her pupils were from the wealthy and influential families of the upper, the aristocratic part of the city, round about Savin Hill and along the Yantic riverside. After she had become established there, she took me back with her at the end of a spring vacation. I found myself among a very different class of children from any I had ever known, highbred, well-mannered and well-dressed, I felt at first abashed and suppressed; but as we were all children, more or less unconscious of distinctions in rank, democrats at heart, I soon came to terms with them; if there were any barriers, they were broken down as soon as we began to play together. There is no realm of equality like that of the playground; there you are estimated on your merits, your skill, your honor and good nature. In two weeks I felt perfectly at home, and already had two or three cronies to whom I was devoted. I dreaded the hour of my return to my mother. It came; I found myself again among men in shirtsleeves, and boys in blue jean overalls; my mother's oven no more busy than of old, my hands black with leather and sticky with wax, I, who had been eating the fine fare of rich men's tables with silver forks and knives that shone like mirrors. The world had been changed in a few weeks and fifty miles of travel. I felt myself no part of anything around me; I loathed it and longed to return to my sister. I had had a taste of better things, or so they seemed, or was it their novelty? I began to look down with shame and disgust at the humble life around me. Above all I wanted to escape my task and wondered how I had ever wished to be a bootmaker.

Norwich was a small and beautiful city, well planted with trees, the houses large and set in ample ground. Two riven meet there to form a third, the Thames, at the head of which is the port or Landing as it is called. At the port of the city I had for the first time seen steamers and sailing vessels. Strange and wonderful creatures they were to me, and I asked a thousand questions about them without comprehending in the least the answers. I was told they sailed down the river with the tide, past New London, then out upon the sea, and at once and ever since I always behold vessels, as it were, double, one near and another far away, disappearing on some vast level plain. Here was water enough, water, the most fascinating thing in nature, tempting by its dangers to boyish adventures, and I determined to be a sailor as soon as I was old enough and could get back to Norwich. How to get back was the problem I vexed myself over day and night for weeks and months. My sister returning home for her summer vacation, I continued to tease and coax until she consented to my wishes. My small trunk, covered with hairy cow hide, was packed with my few belongings, and with a gay heart I left the town and my mother's door never to return permanently, and as blind as a stone to what I was going away for; I was going—that was all that concerned me. There was no future; time does not exist for children; yesterdays are faint, tomorrows undreamed, today endless. Arriving in Norwich, at once, I felt at home. I met my former playmates without a greeting, and just as if we had not been separated for half a year. Nothing was changed; we resumed our sports, and every afternoon at the close of school, in which I was now a pupil, we played among the cedars of Savin Hill; or else we paired off and spent our time with the dogs, rabbits and pigeons and other pets owned by my different companions. I had myself one hen which the good dame, with whom my sister and I boarded, allowed me to keep in a large box in her yard. I spent much of my time, when without companions, with my hen. I made her many nests in hopes of enticing her to lay eggs, for which I was promised a cent apiece by dame Onion. I cannot recall how I came by this hen, nor what was her final fate. What trifles we pursue! What trifles connect the seven ages of life, more often remembered than the real steps of our career. So let biddy spread her wing as wide as Jove's eagle, and eat gravel with Juno's peacock; and in this narration I keep company with my betters, who have not lowered their dignity by confessing their obligations to the beasts of the field, the birds of the air and to all those friendly creatures which dwell in the shelter of the house and the barnyard. So, little red hen, I leave thee here on the road by which I strayed, playing and singing, into the fearful arena of life, walled and thousand-eyed; whether we fall or triumph, the spectacle and the wonder of an hour.

Whether it were better to be the limpet fixed to its rock, forever free from change, or the wild gull soaring over shores and sea, now wading in the mud, now riding gloriously on the crest of the billows, is a query which has often agitated me since the time I abandoned the home of my childhood. For me there was no return now to the rock. I thought of my home with a gloomy dread lest I should have to return to it. Such forebodings, however, were rare and did not interfere with my complete enjoyment of present pleasures. Along with them I caught the manners of the little aristocrats of my sister's school. It was an ideal company of boys and girls, handsome, refined and innocent. My sister herself was a natural lady and rigorous in her demands for perfect conduct on the part of her pupils. She spared me least of all, as more needing such discipline, and also, I suppose, that she might escape any suspicion of sisterly partiality. I have ever been extremely open to personal influences and environment, and apt to take on the customs and opinions of those with whom I mingle. What one gains so is a part of his education. It is true there is a lurking danger as well as advantage, and we may be wrecked or carried into a safe harbor according to the accidents of life and the power or feebleness of the will. My good fortune was seemingly great at this time, having such a sister to watch over me and such influences around me. On the other hand I was disqualified by it for living the life of a poor man which circumstances have made imperative; and it required many years to reconcile me to my lot and to discover other riches by which a man might make his life honorable and happy. My sister's pupils were affectionately attached to her and this feeling was soon shared by their parents. She visited among them continually, and always took me with her. I saw the inside of the houses of the rich, the leading citizens of Norwich, governors and ex-governors of the state, senators, the Rockwells, Greens, Tylers, Williams, Backuses, Lusks, and others, and became used to the elegancies and luxuries of their households. My sister seemed to be recognized as their equal, as well she might be. She was a woman to win her way anywhere; distinguished looking, full of tact and efficiency. She was tall, with a perfect figure and graceful movement. Her eyes were large and dark, her hair black and abundant, in this being the only one of my mother's children who resembled her, as she did also in the contour of her face and nose. She was of a hopeful and joyous temperament and full of energy; by this latter gift she had raised herself from the humblest position to one of influence and acquired in no long time much reputation as a remarkably successful teacher, and her services were in constant demand. She was also a favorite in all classes of society and knew how to adjust herself to the humblest and the highest of her fellow creatures. From the time of her father's death she had been the prop of the family, the mover in all their plans and the provider of their needs. Over me she had a special charge and a sacred duty, for my father, conscious of the too gentle nature of his wife and the poverty in which he was about to leave her, had on his deathbed, committed, had indeed made a solemn gift of his little boy to the daughter whom he trusted most; and for fifty years did she fulfil that trust. On her tombstone are engraved these brief but true words: "Faithful daughter, sister, friend, teacher." New England has been full of such devoted, self-sacrificing daughters and sisters, and still is. I do not single her out as exceptional, but to give her the tribute she merits, and that she may not be among the uncounted and unremembered where these pages shall be read.

In my sister's school besides good manners, which now seem to me the best part of my education, I learned to draw and to sing; and in which I delighted most, it were hard to say. Never before had I heard any music, except that of the doleful and droning church choir. We sang simple songs about nature, conduct, duties to the Heavenly Father, to parents and teacher. Their notes lingered in my ears for a great many years, and I can still hum some of them. We drew plain figures, blocks, cones, the sides and roofs of buildings and outlines of trees. In penmanship I made no progress, and it was always unformed and illiterate until I was a man, and took it in hand without a teacher. My two years' detention from school did not seem to put me into classes below me in age. I could read and spell very well. There were other longer or shorter periods when my education was entirely interrupted; yet I did not have to begin my studies exactly where I had left off. Something carries us along unconsciously and a natural intelligence bridges over the superficial differences between ourselves and our associates. How often have I deceived myself into thinking I knew something when it was merely a borrowed acquirement, as it were, a cuticular absorption from a transient environment or interest, from classmates, social circles, clubs and books. Great books are the most flattering deceivers of all. I never read one that did not touch me nearly in this way. The fall to my own proper level is painful, but has been somewhat stayed and alleviated by reading another. Being of this plastic, imitative nature, I soon took on the manners and childish ideas of my companions in my sister's school. I was already aristocrat enough to look down with indifference upon the boys of the Landing and other parts of the town, and at a good safe distance, to call them by some insulting name. We never came to blows, nor ever nearer than a stone's throw. By the natural elective affinities, which seem to be more marked among boys and girls than among men and women, I formed the closest intimacy with two brothers about my own age. They belonged to the leading family among my sister's patrons. Their father was a wealthy, retired manufacturer who had held every honor Norwich had to bestow. The boys were indulged in all their wishes, in every kind of pet animal that walks or flies, a menagerie of small creatures in cages, ponies for the saddle and dogs to follow. In these I was allowed to share as if my own, and their house was as much mine as theirs, more often taking supper in it than at my boarding place. Thus becoming familiar with and possessing the pleasures which wealth can furnish a boy, I knew not what a fall I was preparing for myself when the thread of my destiny should lead me back into its narrow and tortuous path. How is any one responsible for such passages in his life which carry him into situations and form in him tastes and propensities that must be relinquished with much sorrow or maintained with peril? But the hour of doom was not yet, and my pleasant days had no omen that their sun would ever set. In truth that sun has never set on the days when I was in the company and close beside the one girl in my sister's school with whom I felt the passionless, but none the less ardent delight. Laugh who will—"Her sweet smile haunts me still." Never was sweeter or more captivating on the face of a girl or woman, and it was perpetually there, whether she spoke or only looked in your eyes. By it I should even now recognize her among a thousand. If I had then known that souls are reincarnated, I should have known by her smile that she was the Launa Probana of my earliest awakening. I never played with her, but I was in the same class; she was at the head of it in spelling exercises, where, in the then customary manner, we went up when we mastered a word missed by the pupil below. I was always struggling to stand next to her, and when I did, I was happy. That is how I learned to spell so well! I had become diffident with girls and as much more so with her as I was fond of being with her. Consequently we spoke to each other but little. To be where she was was enough. Those inclinations and awkward attentions, which betray the situation to the onlooker, I manifested always in her presence without suspicion of being observed. I was alert to win her notice by any sort of indirection, and embarrassed to speechlessness when I had won it. There were certain occasions when I could count on having her for my companion, when we found ourselves together by some inevitable attraction. These were on the excursions which my sister was fond of taking with her whole school to places of interest in the vicinity of Norwich. The holiday freedom, the excitement, made it easier for me to be more demonstrative than usual toward the new-found Launa. Yet we were still too young and sensitive for indulgence in the physical tokens of affection. We often walked hand in hand, yet under cover of that which was a permissible and usual gallantry among all the children of the school, the secret attachment of any pair was pleasantly and sufficiently hidden even from themselves. Wondrous were the places we visited; places of historic or natural interest; to Groton by steamboat, where we saw Fort Griswold and its monument to the heroes of the Revolutionary fight, and its still surviving heroine, Mother Bailey, who tore up her petticoat to make cartridges for the gunners. We called upon the venerable woman in her neat, little cottage. She was very proud of her fame. She related the story of the fight, not omitting her part in it. 'Do you think I am a very old woman?" she said to us. "Well, see," and in an instant she was whirling around the room in an old fashioned jig. Then we returned to the Fort, and in its enclosure we opened our baskets and ate our cakes and apples. I sometimes think that was the happiest day of my life. Certainly it was the very beginning of what is called seeing the world. What, is not the first steamboat ride, and with your sweetheart, the first fort, the scene of a battle and the most celebrated heroine of the Revolution something? My sweetheart was the only thing not entirely novel; her smiles ever recalled the memory of Launa Probana. All the way home we stood on deck, leaning over the rail, watching the swirl and foam from the paddle wheels, and our tongues were loosened. As usual, in my attempts at seeming superior to girl companions, I undertook to explain things about which I knew nothing. Now, any boy could put me down in a minute with, "how big you talk;" but my gentler hearer led me on with her acquiescence and her trusting, wondering eyes. The teacher's brother was somebody in her estimation; he was a new kind of boy. The other boys she had known all her life, commonplace, tiresome teasers or clowns. That awkward impediment, a rival, I had not to contest or fear. All went well with us until I fell from the ranks of the aristocracy and became a menial shop boy in a store. But before that eclipse there were other happy days and joyous experiences. Together we visited the grave of the Indian Uncas, and the remnant of his tribe at Montville; we drove often to Fishville, where was an estate laid out in a foreign fashion with grottoes, mazes, fountains, strange trees and shrubbery and a museum of curiosities.

Doubtless it was not the intention of my sister at this time to educate me. Perhaps she saw nothing in me worthy of it. I do not much wonder at her conviction, if such it was, as I look at a daguerreotype of myself taken about that period, a round head, mostly hair, a low forehead, a pair of round eyes, thick nose and lips and short neck, altogether just such a solid, stolid child as one would expect to see from the country, bred in the sun and cold, and fed on brown bread and milk. My being with my sister, and a pupil in her school was a temporary expedient until a place could be found for me. At length it was found, a situation in a dry goods store, where I could earn my board and clothing. Thus without warning I fell completely out of the ranks of the elect and again returned to servitude as a shop boy, a runner of errands, a builder of fires and floor-sweeper.

SHOP BOY

In country stores the man or boy behind the counter was an enviable person. Many boys had no higher ambition than to be a store-keeper. I was now behind the counter, and although there was nothing in a dry goods shop to interest me as in the country store, with its varied assortment of goods, tools, crockery and candies, I felt rather proud of my position, especially when permitted to wait on a customer. He seemed an inferior sort of a person, and I had no idea at first of conciliating him and making a sale. It was not then the custom to observe a fixed price and simply show the goods; but clerks were expected and instructed to use persuasion, to expatiate on quality and beauty, and to take less than they first asked. The cost price was marked with secret characters; the selling price was variable. The more you could get out of a gullible customer, the better; and he who could get the most was the smartest clerk. A thrifty purchaser would beat down the price little by little, the sharp clerk yielding with many protestations until a last offer was made, when, with feigned hesitation, the clerk would wrap up the goods. One thinks he has bought a cheap bargain, the other figures the profit and laughs in his sleeve. It was not my particular duty to wait upon customers except in a rush of trade, or early in the day before the other clerks had arrived. I opened the store in the morning, swept the floors and sidewalk, dusted the counters, filled the lamps, and in winter built the fire. During the day I ran on errands, delivered goods and was the fag of the proprietor and his two clerks. I soon chafed under the confinement, and when sent out of the store I made no haste to return; the farther away the bundle was to be delivered the better I liked it, and I always took the longest way, loitering about, making acquaintance with strange boys, dogs and any wayside apple or pear tree. If possible I skirted the region of the wharves and the rivers, where I always found something interesting going on, a vessel arriving or leaving, sailors chaffing and fighting. Sometimes I received a small fee for delivering the bundle at the door of a lady, but this happened rarely; it was not the custom, and seldom was I even thanked. I had only two memorable adventures on my travels; one was an attack on my breeches by a savage dog, and the other—shall I confess it—almost as disagreeable. A young and handsome woman, whom I had often seen in the store, and knew me, I imagine, better than I knew her, called me into the house with my package, set me on her knees, petted and kissed me, and asked me a lot of questions about one of the clerks. I have reason to believe her tender behavior was meant rather for her beloved clerk than for me. I reported nothing on my return, only, on being reproved for my long absence, I said, "Miss— had kept me," which made the clerk look sheepish. I was not sent to her house again. The clerks, however, did use me a good deal as an innocent pander in their various intrigues with the pretty and fast girls of the town. I carried notes, concealed in dry goods bundles, and brought back answers in my jacket pocket, which I was instructed to deliver on the sly.

The proprietor of the store to whom I was bound, and in whose family I lived, was a tall, thin, sallow-faced man. He had a nervous manner, but he was not unkind to me. He clothed and fed me well. He chewed tobacco and was brimming over with funny stories, funny and usually indelicate. I heard much swearing, too, and I began to think it the proper thing to try to be wicked myself. I was greatly attached to the two clerks, and they were my models in everything. One of them was also the bookkeeper of the establishment as well as a salesman. He dressed after the mode in trig, close-fitting suits; his pantaloons were like tights, and only kept on his legs by straps under his boots. He played and fooled with me in idle hours. The other clerk was exceedingly sober, often melancholy, seldom smiled and had nothing to do with me, rarely speaking to me. I stood in awe and admiration of him. He wrote poetry for the local newspaper, and I think he felt above us all, and above his position. He belonged to a distinguished family, and why he happened to be a dry goods clerk I never knew. He seemed as much out of his natural place as I. How restless and penned up I felt at times no words can tell. The lean dog with freedom, is much more to be envied than the chained dog with a golden collar. It was a small store of only three counters, and during unoccupied hours there was nothing on the shelves or in drawers with which I could amuse myself. In mere desperation for something to occupy myself I counted spools of cotton and silk, unrolled and rolled again pieces of goods, and many a hot summer afternoon, when both the shops and the streets were deserted, I caught flies and put them in a bottle, and then smoked them to death.

I now seldom saw my former playmates. Their families traded at a much larger and more fashionable store. Our customers were of an humbler class, mainly from the suburbs and adjoining villages. But a boy does not long remain companionless, be there another boy within reach. I became intimate first with a lad in a grocery store, whereby there was considerable access to sugar, raisins and other sweets; through him, together with others in similar situations, I was made a member of their secret society, having been tested as to strength, reliability and other qualifications. Our badge was a red morocco star, worn under the left lappet of the vest. The only purpose of the club that I could ever discover, was to lick every boy who did not belong to it! I was expected to celebrate my initiation by challenging three non-members, which I proceeded to do, licked two and met my match in the third. Then I was warned to attack only boys smaller than myself. The morals of the club were meant to be on a par with those of much older boys, but signally failed. We were as bad as we knew how to be; none of us had the courage or the enterprise to do the naughty things which so excited our emulation in our elders. However, we insulted and beat all the goody-good boys in our way, swore small oaths, smoked and swaggered until sick with nausea, and crowning achievement, learned what a Tom and Jerry tasted like, enticed merely by the name. It was not until we had Ike Bromley for a leader, that we fairly succeeded in being as bad as we wished. He had an instinct for mischief and deviltry, and a way with him that led captive the heart and devotion of all boys. Daring and cool, he could carry a sober, innocent face which would disarm a detective and charm a deacon. Whoever got caught or punished, he always escaped. No one could have guessed at this time that he would become one of the most brilliant journalists of his day, the wittiest and most engaging of men at a dinner table, a boon companion, and beloved friend. Money was very scarce with us; what little we had we earned in various outside ways, in doing extra errands or selling old rubbers, old boots, copper and brass. In fact we were the scavengers of the town, and had the run of all the cellars. We managed to sneak or steal our way into most of the shows that visited the town. For some reason, now quite incomprehensible, the wharves were our most common rendezvous. And for what object we spent our small funds on raw clams, eaten out of the shell, and doused with pepper sauce, (which, for my part, I could with the greatest difficulty swallow, bringing tears to my eyes, and burning in my throat for a week after), I as little know, but now suppose it was in imitation of the rough men and sailors about the piers with whom we consorted, and whom we wished to impress with our manliness. Indeed, with all the rough characters about the streets we made friends and aped their manners as much as we could, two or three notoriously fast, rich young men being our particular heroes. Nothing saved us from the realization of our ideals but our extreme youth and native innocence, and perhaps some lurking sense that we were playing at vice, with fire that would not burn and water that would not drown. There was one thing we were ambitious to do, yet could not screw our courage to the sticking point; we wanted to get drunk to see how it felt. Either a Tom and Jerry had not sufficient potency, or we could never find the bottom of the glass before our stomachs rebelled, for we only paid the penalty in a penitential headache without the fun of the debauch.

I realized all the while the peril of my ways in case they should come to light, which only served to increase the excitement, though now and then I had some serious moments. Several times I barely escaped discovery, and our pranks often defied punishment because of our number and the ease with which we could shoulder off the blame on one another. I now thought of the children of my sister's school, with whom I had recently been so intimate, with contempt as far beneath me in knowing how to have real sport.

Although I continued to be the menial of the store, I had acquired some knowledge of the business; could snap a piece of broadcloth to show its firm quality and nap, hang dress goods in proper folds over my arm to give an idea how they would look when made up, and talk quite glibly on the cheapness of our wares in comparison with those of our competitors. I could see that the small boy in a jacket, and only two heads higher than the counter, amused the men customers with his brag attempt at being a salesman, and that the women smiled down upon him approvingly—all of which he took as a compliment to his success; for successful he often was, to the surprise of the older clerks. With what pride did I enter my sales on a slate kept for the purpose under the cash drawer. I surmised that the women sometimes bought goods just to encourage the boy. The clerks laughed and made fun of me telling me it was my rosy cheeks that sold the goods. Young ladies frequented the shop for no other purpose than to chat and flirt with the clerks, and one I remember always kissed me at any favorable chance. How I hated my red cheeks, and tried my best to rub out the color. It was a comfort to be told I should outgrow it, and then the girls would not care for me. For two long years I had ceased to care for them. It was even with some shame that I thought of my Launas, they, who later in life, have formed many an ideal of loveliness.

It is said the child in the womb passes through all animal forms in its growth from the germ to birth. Whether any incipient wings have been observed I have not heard. In much the same way the boy represents in his growth the different stages of civilization from the savage to the civilized man. Some time the average boy typifies the Indian, the cowboy, prizefighter, pirate, sailor soldier; and all classes of rough, wild men are wonderfully attractive to him. He wishes to be like them and plays at being one of them. For more than a year I was greatly attached to the ruffians on the wharves, and to such of the Montville Indians as I could make friends with. A wandering party of Indians from the Penobscot tribe had their tents pitched for a whole summer just outside the city, with whom I became intimate, and spent my leisure time with them. I made my errands go their way, however long the circuit. I should have gone away with them, would they have had me. To live in a tent and shoot with a bow became to me the ideal of life. Strange it is that the most vivid memory of that episode remaining with me is the peculiar smell of the Indians; but it was not then offensive to me.

All these propensities were greatly stimulated by reading at this time the Wandering Jew of Eugene Sue. I had found the volume, a paper covered pamphlet edition, in a drawer in the store. I carried it home secretly and read it at night. After I was supposed to be in bed and asleep, and the house still, I used to get up, partly dress, light my lamp and read often until midnight or as long as the oil held out. I doubt if any one knows the supreme pleasure and excitement of reading, who has not read a book surreptitiously. All the mysteries and horrors of the Wandering Jew entered into my soul, and while it opened a scene and actions utterly new to me, it sobered me far beyond anything that had ever happened to me. About the same time I had many gloomy days and nights of terror from having seen the bodies of twenty-five drowned passengers from the wreck of a steamboat which plied between Norwich and New York City. Our poet clerk took me with him to see them the morning they were brought to the dock on another steamboat of the same line. They were laid out in rows on the main deck, frozen stiff, for it was the winter season, covered with sand and particles of ice, their flesh dreadfully lacerated and blue, their features contorted into ghastly shapes. Among them were two men whom we knew well, frequenters of our store. I clung to the hand of the clerk, and should have fainted, had he not taken me away immediately. He himself was overcome, and his sad face was sadder and longer for many days. The whole city was in gloom and mourning. A revival, which was in progress in one of the Baptist churches, added greatly to its converts in consequence of the accident, and the presence of death in such near and fearful form.

PISTOL MAKER

At length Fortune took a new turn at her wheel. Suddenly the store door closed behind me; broom, oil can, coal hod and scissors knew me no more. I rejoiced in my release and in the prospect of new scenes, new faces and pleasures. What was to be my occupation did not give me one thought; I had as yet no choice, no preference. Wherever there were boys was my world and my trade.

Two of my sister's influential patrons, who had been instrumental in bringing her to Norwich, removed their business to Worcester, Mass. She followed them, and, as usual, I followed her. The business of her patrons was the manufacture of pistols, a patented, six-barrelled, self-cocking revolver, the first of its kind, I believe, ever invented, and a wonder in its day. The whole six barrels revolved on a rod running through their center, and by one and the same ratchet movement the hammer was raised and the chambers of the barrel thrown into position to receive the discharge from a percussion cap. There was a great demand for these pistols in the South and West. It was, I suppose, on account of my sister's intimacy with the families of these manufacturers that a place was found for me in their works.

See me now no longer in a linen shirt and brown broadcloth jacket, but again in blue jean overalls, with grimy, oily hands and dirty face, shut in walls from which was no escape for ten hours each day. The lathes, hand tools, forges and engine which operated the machinery were novel and interesting to me at first. I was the only boy in the establishment. The workmen, all skilled mechanics, were a remarkably fine body of men. They earned large wages, lived quite comfortably, and were prominent in their several circles and churches. One of them became Lieut. Gov. of Mass. I was placed under the charge of the foreman of the first floor where the heavier part of the material of the pistol was prepared. I did the odd jobs of the room, worked a punching machine and managed the lathe that turned the rough outside of the pistol barrel. My master took an active personal interest in me and was very minute and painstaking in his instructions. He was a very pious man and lost no opportunity of exhorting me to seek religion and become converted. It made no impression on me; I understood no word he said. Besides, just the same words had always been familiar to me and had never conveyed any meaning to my simple ears. It did not trouble me to be called a sinner; it never occurred to me to question whether I was or not. In short in my innocence and indifference, I was a perfect type of the thing itself, as understood by the church. But when my master invited me to go a-fishing on some half holiday, that was a very different sort of a text, which I well understood. Alas, when the fish did not bite, it gave an uncomfortable opportunity for a little exhortation. In addition to the work in the shop I spent much time in the office, where I was employed in putting the last touches to the pistols before being packed for delivery. I burnished the silver plates, set in the handles, cleaned and oiled the chambers, hammers and nipples, and polished the whole with fine chamois skin. Thus I had a hand in the beginning and completion of the construction of a pistol, and knew pretty well all the intermediate operations. I also obtained an inkling of the way the business was conducted by hearing the conversation and discussions of the proprietors. I heard many secrets. Some of them confused my small glimmerings of moral sense. It seemed to me that I had known the same sort of obliquities among boys in the swapping of jacknives. I heard the bookkeeper say one day, "business is business; this is no Sunday school." I had bewildering thoughts. Was it possible these pistols were not what they seemed and would not kill a man? For I knew they were sold mostly in the South for the fighting of duels. I longed to try one on a cat. The sun rose and set on my suspicions, with never a solution. To this day I cannot rid myself of an innate doubt when I make a purchase. I expect to be cheated.

I seemed in a fair way at last of acquiring a trade, and it might have been, except for the accident of my boarding place. For there I first came in contact with books and students. It was not a regular boarding house, save for three months in the winter. I was taken into the family on account of its association with mine long before in Bellingham. The master of the house had formerly been the clergyman of that town, but was now a botanic-eclectic physician and general medical professor of a school, which held one winter session in his house. It was attended by only a dozen students. Lobelia was Prof. —'s strong point. Everybody in the house was put through a course of lobelia with a heavy sweat, sometimes to cure a slight indisposition, but more often as an experiment. My only escape from the drudgery of the workshop was in feigning sickness and undergoing the Professor's panacea. This confined me to the bed for a day and gave me another day for recovery, when I could be about and enjoy myself. These sweatings and retchings took the color out of my cheeks so that when I returned to the shop it was easily believed that I had been ill, and, with considerable sympathy, my master also warned me of the brevity and uncertainty of life and the necessity of preparing for the day of wrath. Little did he know how all this could be escaped by a good dose of lobelia.

It was a curious life I led at this time between my regular occupation, lobelia, the dissecting room of the professor and frequent religious exhortations. I was immensely delighted by the secrets of the basement cellar, where, in winter, the cadavers were kept I became accustomed to the sight of them, and frequently inspected them when alone, curious to see the internal structure of a human body, for until that time I was not conscious of any internal structure of the human body. Hands and feet were the epitome of my physiology. The whole business of dissection was conducted in the most clandestine manner, although the subjects were obtained from Boston and were, no doubt, honestly procured. There was probably some professional reason for their being all women. I know not why, but I seemed to be trusted by the Professor and his little band of students, and when cadavers arrived at the railroad station by express, I was often sent to watch them until they could be removed. They came in large casks packed in oats.

I had little time to make acquaintance with boys, as I was not allowed on the street in the evening, and Sunday was strictly observed. Nor did I know any girls of my own age. With the pretty waitress of the Professor's dining-room, some years older than myself, I had occasional ardent encounters on back stairs and in dark entries. I was less embarrassed by them than formerly and began to play the beau. As usual, only girls much older than myself attracted me. I began to have the same experience with regard to men. There were even some moments when I dimly realized why some men were respected and honored. For the proprietors of the pistol factory I had a deep reverence. One of them, the inventor of the self-cocking pistol, was the model of a reserved, dignified gentleman. I saw much of him in the office attending to his business, deciding and despatching it with few words. The other member of the firm was in complete contrast to his partner. His round, jolly face was always wreathed in smiles, a joke, a pun, or story always forthcoming, and business the last thing to be considered. He was a college graduate and a poet of local reputation. It is singular in my boyhood how often I happened to be dropped in the vicinity of small poets. This gentleman was, like myself, a native of Bellingham, and on that account he sometimes noticed me and made inquiries after my well-being. He seemed to me a very great man, chiefly because he wrote poetry and had it printed in books. I imagine that he expected me to remain a mechanic, and had little thought of the influence he was unconsciously exerting over the future. Nor did I myself recognize it, until years later when my first article appeared in a magazine; feeling some pride in this grand, world-moving effort, I sent it to him as a lawful tribute. Time had not been kind to him; he had almost lost the use of his hand for writing and was using some sort of mechanical contrivance for that purpose. But the fire of the proselyter still burned in him, and he ended his note of acknowledgment with the old familiar query about the salvation of my soul.

THE AWAKENING

Having no boy associates I began to cultivate the Professor's students. I spent my leisure time with them, and, through their conversation, entered a new world. Words are too cold a medium to convey the change that came over me, for at the same time that I began in some measure to appreciate the learning and general knowledge of these young men I began to be conscious of my own ignorance, I became aware that I knew nothing, never had, and probably never should. Consequently I was more depressed than stimulated. I reflected on the conversations I heard among the students, and the pithy, sententious sayings of the Professor at the table. He usually settled all discussions and table talk with a witticism or apt quotation, I was about to say with a toothpick; for he had a curious habit of digging his thumb and finger into his vest pocket and fumbling for one, jabbing it into one side of his mouth and delivering his wisdom from the other side. His wife who sat opposite to him, tall, lean and prim always frowned on any levity at the table. It was her opinion that we should eat our food in silence and as quickly as possible, so that, as she often remarked, the table could be cleared and the kitchen work not be delayed. To her great distress the conversation often became so lively that the meal dragged, and various were her devices for bringing back our attention to the business at hand. I had some sense of the humor of the situation, and as I never took part in the talk, I amused myself by exchanging winks with the pretty waitress. She was the only person in the house near my own age. We were very good friends; she cut me a little larger piece of pie than she served to the others, darned my socks and called me "Sonny," and "curly head." She was not averse to an arm around her waist, and I repaid her kindness in the only currency I had—a kiss. However, I more enjoyed the society of the students than I did hers. I could be in their company without being noticed. No word escaped me and slowly, then, at length, overwhelmingly, there was borne in upon me the crushing sense of the difference between these young men and myself, their interests, expectations, future careers and mine. Yet I saw no way out of my present situation. The bitter seeds of unrest, and ambitions without opportunities, were at the same time planted in a fruitful soil. When the soul of man is awakened, not one but all its faculties awaken together. Hitherto the memory of my past life had no existence and no interest. It was a blank page.

All at once, when most cast down and discouraged in my thought of the future, that blank page of the past became illuminated and full of delightful pictures and memories. I was entirely overcome by them. They all pointed back to Bellingham, which I had not thought of since leaving it. The attraction to the place became irresistible. It seemed as if there I could recover myself and begin my life over again, continuing all its joys, reuniting all its companionships. It is obvious to me now that this was an evasive yet ingenuous effort to escape from myself, an awakening that had come to me, which I knew not how to meet. I revolved several plans for getting back to my native place and becoming a farmer. None of these were practicable, and I determined to go, trusting to chance to make the way plain. But even the going had difficulties. I solved them by setting out. I crossed the bridge before I came to it, and all the way was easy. I could take no scrip for the journey, for I had none; neither two coats, for I had but one; nor yet could I take the blessing of any one, for to no one save the waitress did I entrust my intentions. I set out on foot, and once on the road, I felt as free and joyous as a bird. There were twenty-five miles to cover, and I expected to do them from sun to sun of a late April day. Sometimes I ran for a mile or two from sheer eagerness to arrive. Most of the way I sauntered along thinking of nothing, overflowing with animal spirits.

Enough the freedom, the open sky, the earth, which had been lost to me for three years. It did not occur to me that I was running away, not from outward conditions, but from myself; that at last I had come to the not unusual crisis in the life of boys. However, it was a very mild form of runaway, twenty-five miles, and its objective my old home; not the lure of the sea nor the army, nor yet the adventures of the dime novel hidden in the hay mow. No, it was none of these, but strangely in contrast to them, an impulsive, passionate awakening of memory, an attempted escape from a future, which had been shown to me as in a vision, and from which I shrank in fear and despair.

At noon I was half way between Grafton and Upton and I rested on a high bank with my back against a stone wall. There I could see the church spires of Milford town, and beyond, the land fell away toward Bellingham. I ate some food that the waitress had given me for the journey, and took the road again. Soon I was in Milford. The remainder of the way was very familiar. I knew every house, rock and tree; yet everything looked smaller than I anticipated. I hurried on as I wished to arrive at Uncle Lyman's before his supper time, which I knew was invariably at five o'clock the year round. Uncle Lyman's house, to which I was going, was the house in which I was born. He had been my father's most intimate friend. The house had always been like a home to me, even after my family had one of their own. As I hurried along I saw again the house, one-storied, and the elm tree, with its branches extending over the roof, and arching the highway. I suddenly remembered the flat stone that had been set in its bole for a seat, which the tree had so overgrown that, as a child, I could sit there and be almost hidden from sight; and the brook which flowed through the fields near the house, where the grass was always a darker green along its course, even when it dried up; and the windings so many and sharp that they seemed to write letters when one looked down upon them from a little elevation. I have sat in a tree and fancied I spelled out words in the green grass.

As I came nearer the house I became more and more agitated about the welcome that awaited me. It was friendly, yet surprised, and not as warm as I had expected. Had they changed? Or was it I? Certainly I did not feel at home. This was the house most dear to me, this the settle where I had sat when my legs did not reach the floor. How familiar sounded the voices I now heard, one deep and penetrating, the other a thin falsetto; yet I did not feel the comfort I had imagined that I should. At the table were the same dishes I remembered; the taste was gone. After supper I went out and tried to sit in my old seat in the elm. It was too small for me now; alas, it seemed to disown me, to have cast me out. The barn which once looked so enormous appeared insignificant. I went to bed unreconciled and unhappy. Yet how can a healthy boy awake in the morning dejected? Night, pitying night, which knows how the evil days succeed each other, hinders their sad return and hides in her oblivious mantle their weariness, their sorrows and their disappointments. I was awake at dawn, and yesterday was forgotten. The sun shone across the tops of the forest oaks just beginning to show their red buds. There was dew on the grass and a sweet, earthy smell in the air. Robins were calling everywhere and blue birds flying low from fence to fence. The little brook was full to the brim; the lush grass laid flat along its borders. I found the places where I used to erect my miniature mill wheels, and the remains of the little dam. Here was already antiquity. I did not need Egypt or Greece. Childhood contains their whole story. The season was unusually early; the great elm was becoming misty with the ruffled edges of its unfolding leaves. The outermost sprays began to drop from increasing weight of sap and leaf bud. Catkins hung on birch and willow and alder and the ancient bed of tansy had a new growth of three inches. Down the hill toward Beaver Pond, and along the meadow clusters of ferns were leading up their brides and bridegrooms in opposite pairs with bowed heads. It was twenty days before the usual pasturing time; but Uncle Lyman was turning his cattle out for half a day to keep the grass from becoming too rank and sour. I helped him drive the cows, oxen and heifers to the pasture. How they gamboled, kicked up their heels and tossed their heads. No more bow and stanchion, no more dry hay and confinement for them. I shared in their exhilaration, having been myself a prisoner for the past six months, and as we drove them afield, could hardly keep from dancing and shouting. "There, my son," said Uncle Lyman, "let me see if you have forgotten how to put up the bars."

I lifted them into place with a will, and thought, this is the life for me. Emboldened by his question I opened my mind in a roundabout way as to helping him all summer on the farm. He saw my drift at once and told me he could not hire me, nor any other boy; he must have a man if anybody, and that I must stick to my trade.

"You can stay a few days," he continued, "and then you had better go back to it," and as if to soften his advice he added, "The first cloudy day we will try for pickerel, though it is rather too early."

This might have been discouraging and a dreadful check to my plans, but by some sudden transition wholly inexplicable, I had already half given them up. My discontent and melancholy had been exhausted in the running away; and a few hours experience of disenchantment reconciled me to my lot.

There is no human experience more acutely painful than when one awakens to the fact that he is a person, an ego, unrelated to people or things, with no real claim to assert save that of habit or associations. The sense of isolation and loneliness is at first overpowering, and vainly does he try to attach himself to former objects and environment. The awakening may come in mature years, it may come in youth; but at what time it appears, the old heavens and the old earth crumble and the soul faces its own destiny and recognizes that it must walk alone.

I was surprised to see how the face of things had altered, when, in the course of the day, I hunted up the two playmates with whom I had formerly been most intimate. I met a cold reception. We could not find our way back to the old ground, the old innocent relation. As for Launa Probana, I did not so much as inquire for her. Time and change had not yet made her distinct and dear. After this I enjoyed myself very well for a few days, excusing my prank with the notion that it was a vacation. We went fishing, but the pickerel would not come from their hiding places. In the evenings Uncle Lyman and his wife at their several sides of the fireplace, she with her knitting, and he with his pipe, and I in a corner of the settle, talked of the days when my father was alive, and of the labors they underwent to make a good farm, clearing the brush and stones and building the fences. They told me of my birth and my father's joy at having a son. Then when I inquired for Nahum, their son, whom I remembered as a young man, when I was a child, a sudden silence fell over the great kitchen. There was no reply and the mother's head drooped over her work and tears fell upon it. I wondered, but did not dare to speak, and shortly I climbed the attic stairs to my bed. The next day Uncle Lyman cautioned me not to mention Nahum again before his wife. He said he had run away, and they knew not where he was. A guilty pang struck my heart; I became conscious of what I had done, and thought perhaps at that very moment my sister might be weeping for me.

Nothing was now wanting to complete the failure of my escapade, and I was as eager to run back as I had been to run away. Memories, touched by imagination, had come to naught in contact with reality. I learned my first lesson in keeping it and ideals in their proper place. A bird in the bush is worth two in the hand! Utopia is a far country, toward which to travel is better than to arrive. It was some years before I restored the Bellingham of my imagination. If experience be nothing but suffering then I had experienced; over this transaction therefore I grant an act of oblivion.

The return to Worcester was tedious. I was in no hurry, dreading my reception; what should I say, what should I answer? I revolved many explanations, but each I could think of contained a falsehood. With all my waywardness I was never a good liar; the lie was manifest in my face and I could feel it there as something not myself. I concluded to say nothing and not attempt any apology. This proved the wiser plan. Few questions were asked; reproachful looks were to be expected. Some penalty I paid in the shop also; harder tasks were set for me and I was kept more strictly to my work. The students of Prof. Lobelia were now gone, the sessions of his medical school closing in April, and the house seemed lonesome. In the course of the summer there came into the family a young man who was preparing himself to be a missionary. For the first time I heard of Greek and Latin books. The young man was studying both; it excited my curiosity. Here were other things of which I knew nothing, and I began at this period to be oppressed continually by the more and more frequent discovery of the extent of my ignorance. Luckily I knew how to read. My rustic mentors had warned me against girls, but never of books. I found in the Professor's library a queer assortment of odds and ends of learned works. There was a shelf of theology and missionary records, doubtless collected when he was a minister; many shelves of medical books, and a small number of miscellaneous works, histories and cyclopaedias. Among these latter I chanced one day to take down Whelpley's Compend of History. All that I can remember of it now are its stories of ancient heroes, Alexander, Caesar, the greater and lesser men of Greek and Roman annals. That of Alexander made the deepest impression upon me; I know not why, perhaps his conquests, his glory, his youth. I scarcely knew before what the word hero meant. It was a mark of utter inexperience and a visionary temperament that my ambition should have been so aroused by the career of an ancient hero instead of the man who had invented a self-cocking pistol. It was to be two thousand years behind the times, in an age when half a generation is sufficient to write you down as belated and not wanted. However, it is well to have a hero in youth, an example, a spur, a Bucephalus, although one gets many a fall before he reaches the goal, and I can date my desire to know more and to achieve something from the reading of that brief compend of ancient history.

If ever a man finds a path to the true life, he experiences two awakenings, the intellectual and the spiritual, and it matters little which is first. In Worcester I stumbled upon the two books in the space of three years, which led me from darkness to day. The first was that I have just described; the other was of somewhat the same character, Emerson's Representative Men.

The beech at last divides the rock in whose invisible seam its tiny seed was sown. I now began to spend all my leisure time in reading, and to be more and more aware of my unprofitable and aimless life. Books carried me this way and that. I was wholly overcome by them as by a strong personal influence, especially when I read Byron. The student whom I have mentioned had a few books of poetry, and among them the complete works of Byron in one thick volume bound in calf, and printed on cheap, thin paper. He himself had written verses before his conversion. He now looked upon his poets as witnesses of his former sinful state. He wanted to sell them to me with all their sins, and eventually I did buy his copy of Byron for fifty cents, after borrowing and becoming so enamoured of it that I felt I could not live without the book. The Byronic moods and fashion I imitated to the best of my ability. I began to turn down my Sunday linen collar which had stood up to my ears, and to wear my hair long and careless; whereas formerly, I had brushed it back and upward as straight as possible, after the manner of ministers and school-masters, now I let it hang as it would over my forehead and neck. Melancholy was the wear, and for this, in my present temper, not much effort was required. I did not, as Alexander and Chrysostom had done, put my favorite author under my pillow; but often having to sleep on the floor, this volume of Byron served as my pillow. In turn one book after another held me like a captive lover, and I endeavored to conform my life to what I read, no sooner enthralled by one than I found another more enchanting. I formed a taste for reading that has lasted all my life, in which, if there be any education, any mental discipline, is the only consistent part of my development. Our critics and literary mentors extol such books as are fit to be read a second time. I have a still better reason for a second reading, because I forget the first. When I strictly examine myself I cannot say that the contents of any book remain long with me, not even the Greek and Latin grammars over which I spent years of terrible toil. Somewhat survives the years, vague, inexact and never at hand when wanted. Enough for me that I know pretty well where to find what I have once read. I have been drawn to the authors, who have written especially for me, by a certain, recurrent impulse and appetite. Then I can go to the shelf in the dark. I find that memory is a faculty over which we cannot use the whip and spur to much purpose. It goes its own gait through barren or fertile fields, gathering many a weed with its flowers. How many trifles one carries through life from childhood days, by no effort of his own, things of the senses mostly, when these were unwritten tablets and blank for the first impressions. Upon these tablets are indelibly retained a certain box, a spool, a pair of stairs, the smell of a neighbor's house, when, with all my efforts, I cannot recover my father's voice and countenance, nor many another thing that would make a golden treasury of memory. Instead, it is more like the lumber of an old attic, or the contents of a boy's pocket. From much reading I began to observe the difference between written and spoken languages, and to single out the people who used the best speech in their common conversation. I tried myself to talk like the books I read. Never before had I noticed any difference between men as to education. All were on the same plane, only separable by some personal relation to myself. Little by little they became distinct so that I attempted to classify them in a crude and bookish way. Character and the moral point of view, with their manifold applications to life, were as yet hidden from me. I judged men and women by their speech, even by their pronunciation, and thought that I could detect the accent of the educated. In short, education became all in all to my mind; the one desirable possession, and its end the writing of books, its reward fame. As was natural I tried to write, but my rude penmanship, my inability to spell the words, which I was ambitious to use, the difficulty of beginning a sentence, and still greater perplexity of ending it, completely disgusted me and filled me with despair. It was more evident than ever that education was the ladder for my enterprise. There was, at that time, in Worcester a learned blacksmith, who knew fifty languages; he might have been an example to me; yet I had never heard of him. I knew only the great men of Whelpley's ancient history, and the poet Byron. Schools and colleges assumed great and greater importance. I saw no way of educating myself: I expected it to be done for me, as everything thus far had been. I was nearly sixteen years old, barely able to read and write, but no more advanced than the average boy of ten or twelve.

STUDENT LIFE

After much solicitation I persuaded my sister to send me for one term to the Worcester Academy. This was a school then in the suburbs of the city under the patronage of the Baptists. It had formerly been a manual labor school; that is, students could pay their expenses by labor on a farm belonging to the institution. This feature had been given up, and it was conducted like other institutions of a similar character. It was essentially a country academy, intended primarily for youths who, having gone through the common schools, desired some further education at small expense. One or two terms were considered sufficient to round off the culture of farmers' sons. The school pretended to teach Latin and Greek, and occasionally sent a student to college. A few, having acquired a taste for study, remained long enough to fit themselves to become teachers of common schools, or to enter one of the professions, which at that time did not place so much importance as at present upon lengthy preparation and a degree. The expenses were as light as was the fare. The rooms were scantily furnished; chairs, tables and beds were in the last stages of dilapidation from the rough usage of a generation of students. No one felt or was held responsible for their condition. Some of the students boarded themselves in the dormitory, which did not add to the tidiness and order of their rooms. Books, clothing, plates and pots, wood and food were scattered about promiscuously. Each room was a citadel, neither teachers nor steward ever entered it; a servant made up the bed, and that was the extent of her function. We filled our own water pails, cut our own wood and swept the room when we happened to think of it, and could borrow a broom. As I have said, the common table was meagerly kept. How could it have been otherwise at the rate of one dollar per week? We often rose in rebellion at the cooking, when we drove the waitress from the room, hurling the food, and after it, the dishes, upon the floor. No punishments ever followed these out-breaks, nor any of our pranks with the bell, the steward's horse and cow and the principal's desk. The discipline was mild; or rather there was none. And yet there were many diligent students and a few who distinguished themselves in later life. The best features of the institution were its unbounded freedom, the close democratic companionship of the students, the affectionate attachments formed, and the tremendous interest we took in the meetings of the Philomathean society for debates, and the reading of essays and poetry, exhibited also in a lesser degree in the Saturday declamations and compositions. How deep and real were our personal attachments I may illustrate in mentioning that I have maintained two of them for fifty years. Others that faded out of my life I still remember with grateful and tender feelings, especially a young man considerably older than myself, to whom I was passionately devoted. He was a handsome, reserved fellow with the eyes and lips of genius. He played the violin, and well do I recall the sensitive twitchings of his mouth at any strain of unusual thrilling sweetness. It made my heart beat faster when he spoke to me, which was rarely; and never before had I felt such a deep emotion as when coming from the city one evening he asked me to take his arm. It was the common custom with all of us when walking or strolling about the grounds to lock arms or put them about each other's necks. Only with him, the violinist, it was less usual than with the others. How often have I wondered what was the subsequent career of him whom we thought the greatest man among us.

With such freedom, such slight discipline, and so little pressure in the classroom, it was nevertheless the best arena for the development of the whole man which I have ever known. Our debates were exciting, often fierce; sometimes we almost came to blows, and instead of being merely practice and forensics, they were very real and vital, so much so, that we generally resumed them when two or three met in their rooms or on their walks. They were sure to continue until the next meeting, when a new question would be proposed. Usually the topics for debate and the principal disputants were selected a week in advance. Much time was given to preparation, to the complete neglect of our studies. The debates were extemporaneous, and after the preliminary speeches, the question was open to all. The topics of debate were generally on the social and political issues of the time; anti-slavery, temperance, women's rights; these questions often led into religious and theological controversies. Not who was the better scholar, but who was the better speaker, and next the better writer, was the popular estimate of reputation and settlement of rank in school. We strove above everything to be eloquent, to become orators; that being at the time the aim set before us by ambitious public men, inspired by the examples of Webster, Clay, Calhoun and others. It is my belief that, at this period, one of the great public prizes of glory, which young students set before themselves, was to deliver a Fourth of July oration. Meanwhile no instruction was given in elocution, rhetoric or composition. The required exercises in declamation and writing were conducted with almost no criticism. They neither added nor subtracted from our standing with the teachers by any sign known to us. We were left to our own self-instruction, which, on account of our enthusiasm, emulation and rivalries, was the very best of school-masters. We studied parliamentary law from a little volume called Cushing's manual; for who could tell when he might be called upon to be an officer of the club, or at what point he could with safety move the previous question? Very amusing were some of the attempts of the students to speak extemporaneously; the stammering, the hesitation, the confusion and final flunk; the confidence with which some one would spring to his feet, as if full to the muzzle, and the entire inconsequence and futility of his words, ending in apparent abject paralysis of speech. We dealt liberally in jeers at any exhibition of bathos or fustian; in laughter and applause at any touch of eloquence or wit. What better training was there than this? I have always had a fond lingering desire to be an orator, but when before an audience found myself as cold as a clod. Toward essay writing and reading our attitude was somewhat different. Yet here we looked for and were only satisfied with eloquence—good, resounding periods with plentiful classical allusion and quotations of poetry. We always expected at least one apostrophe to "Science Hill," which was the consecrated name of the eminence on which the academy building stood. Progress, liberty, the Fathers of the Republic and other patriotic themes were those on which we sharpened our pens. For purely literary subjects there was no interest whatever; and, because of this indifference, occurred what was, to me, one of the most mortifying episodes of my youth. I had come into the possession of Milton's poetry, and though untouched by his Paradise Lost, his Lycidas was a revelation to me of the music and rhythm and allusions possible to poetry. I committed it to memory and startled my class one day by reciting it as a part of the regular exercises. It was customary for some criticism to follow such exercises; but, to my distress, my beautiful poem, that had filled me with delight, was received in absolute silence. It had fallen like a bolt from heaven on those young wights. Covered with confusion, I went to my seat feeling that I had committed the unpardonable sin of attempting to do something beyond my capacity. No comment on my effort was made at the time; I was not even rallied about it outside the class room; and only after fifty years had passed did I learn the reason of the extraordinary silence that had followed my rhetorical outbreak. Said one of my classmates at a reunion, "I shall never forget the day you recited Lycidas; none of the fellows had ever done such a thing; they neither knew nor cared for poetry, and your recitation was a revelation to us all. It came like a shock and thrilled us to bigger things. We never forgot it."

So impressionable and plastic is youth in its formative period that it only takes one great poem to unlock for it the higher mysteries.

We taught ourselves patriotism in season, and before the days of attenuated and hypersensitive politics. Rough fellows were we, dressed in cheap coats, eating coarse food, sleeping on hard beds in cold rooms, and I fear the well was not much called upon for baths. We read but little. There was not a newspaper nor magazine taken in the whole establishment, and how we knew what was going on in the world I cannot tell; yet in some way it penetrated our seclusion. In such a small and socially affiliated school, what one knew, all the others soon imbibed. We were every one of us Yankee boys, acquisitive and resolved to make the most of ourselves and our small opportunities. The library of the institution contained about a hundred volumes, and of these some were religious books. There was a ragged, greasy Shakespeare in eight volumes which I tried to read through, but found the task too much for me. However, I did have a glimpse of something for which I found myself unprepared; and such is the constitution of my mind, that I have seldom been able to grasp dramatic writing with complete enjoyment; I am apt to dwell too long on its beauty spots. For this reason I prefer the Greek drama, because of the simplicity of its construction. The characters are fewer, and, I may say, not so personal, and there are not so many threads to keep in hand. I am in no perplexity when I begin Agamemnon and Antigone; there is a clear, simple and straight path for action. The one book which we all read with greatest diligence was Todd's Student's Manual. As we did not really study much, it seemed best to know all about the methods and rules for study. The book was stuffed full of sound advice in regard to the regulations of the student's time, diet, sleep and exercise; in short, what may, without offense, be called the mechanical apparatus for the acquirement of education and character. I am sure I profited much from this manual, although I could never observe a tithe of its instructions. It was something to know there was a path especially laid out for the student, if he could not always keep it. It prompted the searching of one's self, and in consequence, many of us began to keep a diary, which, I think in my own case, stimulated observation and reflection. Feeble as the young child's first effort to walk were my entries in my first diary. How is one to write without a definite subject, or one selected for him? But with each day's practice it became easier, and at last a pleasure to hold a silent intercourse with myself, to recover and merely to catalogue the day's doings and try to discriminate them. In vain thus far were my attempts at logic in the debating club, and the sentences in my diary seemed even more wanting in connection. Conjunctions would not join, nor any therefores and wherefores tie the sentences. It was merely chance that I landed a verb in the right place, and did not altogether lose the noun. I seemed to know what I wanted to say but it would not form itself on the pen, and what I wrote one day I had an infinite disrelish for the next. I have heard something in my time about rising upon our dead selves. I know of nothing so dead and so precipitating as the look into an early youthful diary. Not much more encouraging is the book one has written and published, and some time after has the temerity to open.

SCHOOLMASTER

After a few terms at Worcester Academy, during which I contrived in different ways to support myself on a single meal a day, at one time by ringing the bell for morning prayers and sweeping the general recitation room, at another by delivering a daily newspaper, the *Worcester Spy*, to one hundred and twenty-five subscribers, I thought myself competent to teach a common school, by which I hoped to earn enough to carry me through another year of study. I was examined as to my qualifications for teaching by the chairman of the school committee of the town of Grafton, having applied for one of the district schools. Between fright and incompetency I passed a most inadequate examination. What little I did know deserted me at the pinch. The reverend gentleman, who conducted me through questions in the various common school studies, was one of the most amiable souls in the world, as I had many subsequent opportunities of knowing, for he continued my friend as long as he lived. He told me frankly that he was hardly warranted in giving me a certificate, but would allow me to make a trial of the school, and, as my sister had such a high reputation as a teacher, he had no doubt I would succeed if I was in earnest and studied diligently. The school consisted of fifty pupils of all ages; some were just learning to read, others had been through again and again all the text books in use and went to school in winter for fun, and because they had nothing else to do. There were six young men four years older than myself. These older pupils thought they knew their school books well enough, and had no occasion to study them again. They were much inclined to match their proficiency with that of their teacher, which was a good way of putting him on his mettle. A few appeared to be present only to make trouble, and to try their pugilism against that of the master. I was not especially athletic; yet, when my temper was up, I was a dangerous antagonist. I soon discovered the work cut out for me. I spent every evening in preparation for the next day's lessons, and I introduced some new exercises for those older boys and girls whose familiarity with their books gave them little to do. My troubles began soon enough, not in the school, but among the parents, which was shortly reflected in their children. In every New England school district there are generally factions and parties as in larger political divisions; it divides on all kinds of issues, political, religious or social. I am giving my experience, not for its personal value, but as the average picture of the average school district. This particular district was sharply split by the temperance party and the rummies. It so happened that the prudential committeeman as he was called, that is, the agent whose office it was to hire a teacher and have the general care of all the business concerns of the school for the year, was an ardent temperance worker and I boarded with him. This was reason enough for the other party to stir up antagonism against the teacher. It was not long before I became aware of the situation, and learned to my surprise and amusement that I was a strong temperance man, and in the habit of making temperance speeches. The rummies, I found, were men addicted only to their cider barrels; hard working citizens with red faces and rather lurid speech. On the whole, I thought them much more interesting characters than the faction to which I was supposed to belong. But they would have none of me, and I had not sufficient tact to win them to myself. The crisis came when I thrashed the son of one of them, my first and last experiment in corporal punishment. The boy's father threatened and sent me word that the first time he met me I might look out for his horse whip. I fully expected it, and carried a stick on my way to and from school. He turned out to be a great coward, for one day we met on the road and he slunk the other side of his load of wood as we came opposite each other. He took his boy out of school, and several others followed him, complaining that I did not know enough arithmetic to teach them, which was quite true, only I was learning; and gladly would I learn and gladly teach, if they could have had patience. I think my most successful teaching has been with those with whom I was also studying and learning, having a double incitement and interest. The teacher who knows it all beforehand, and rests in his knowledge is soon dulled and wearied.

This incident, the thrashing of one boy and the withdrawal of several others, brought peace and good will into the schoolroom, and I became on intimate and even affectionate terms with the remainder of the pupils, and on the last day of the term, examination day it was called, we were all much lauded and flattered by the school committee and assembled friends. It was my first experience of responsibility, and settled some matters with me for life, chief of which was that the only authority and influence of value are those that are gained by love. The more friendly and intimate my relation with any pupil the more pleasant was my task, the more easy his lesson, the more rapid his progress. I also learned that all effort is lost on a stupid mind, and that it is better to wait upon its awakening. In this I had my own experience to support me, for I never learned anything until aroused from within; all else is but untempered plaster that falls away as soon as it ceases to be fresh. Outside of my school and its duties I found considerable opportunity for improving myself. The couple, with whom I boarded, were good souls, and, having no children of their own, showed me much kindly attention. The table was plentiful; we had pumpkin pie three times daily, baked in oblong tins, and the corner piece was the favorite cut. My room was large and pleasant, and better furnished than any I had ever occupied. My host always wore a cheerful smile and seemed the happiest of men, although he never joked; his conversation was serious and religious, in striking contrast to his manner and usual countenance. He spoke of heaven and hell with the same merry twinkle in his eye, the same smiling face. His speech was accompanied by a sort of low, half audible whistle. He encouraged me through all my troubles, and told me not to worry about the old cider-drinking farmers, as there were more horsewhips than one in the "deestrict." His wife's chief dread in this mortal life was fire. She expected the house would burn up every night. I can see now her painful look of alarm when there was news of a conflagration anywhere; she would immediately leave her chair, look at the stove, examine the stovepipe and peer out into the kitchen. Then it was not unusual for dissolute, drinking men to take revenge on the total abstainers by setting fire to their barns. There was only one family in the district with whom I became intimate, and whose friendship across the continent I still keep. This was the family of a retired Universalist clergyman. They lived in a large farmhouse, and the clergyman was engaged in reclaiming an immense bog, and occasionally supplying some vacant neighboring pulpit. He was a visionary of a perfect kind. All bogs were to him prospective gardens of Eden; impossibilities to him the only things worth attempting; all men saints and angels. He had inherited a considerable fortune, which had mostly disappeared in the fathomless swamps of the different towns where he had sojourned as a clergyman. His wife was a lineal descendant of one of the heroes of Concord Bridge; a beautiful, domestic woman full of prudent and wise counsels, which had saved the family from being swallowed up in her husband's Utopias. Three of their younger children were among the brightest of my pupils; three grown up sons were still at home, working on the land a part of the year, and in winter they made boots in a little shop attached to the house. As formerly in Hopkinton, so here in this shop, but with more intelligence and learning, I heard and now took part in the discussion of all sorts of questions. Their minds seemed to have been trained in more philosophical directions than any I had met. Here I had some new insights which helped me forward, and I heard much of the worthlessness of religious dogmas. It was, however, with a tin pedler, a friend and distant relative of this family, that I turned the newest leaf in my mental progress. He usually travelled through Grafton twice a month, and made it his convenience to put up over night with his friends. It was there I used to meet him. His name was Daboll, and he claimed to be descended from that ancient

Connecticut maker of arithmetics and almanacs, Nathan Daboll. He said that was why he became a pedler—he was born to calculate. Yet his occupation sat very lightly upon him. It gave him abundant opportunities for reflection and conversation. In the latter he took delight, and lost no chance of displaying his skill in setting forth his own ideas and drawing out those of his customers. If he sold a pan or a broom it was accompanied by some bit of philosophy that he had evolved on the lonesome stretches of road between farmhouse and farmhouse. I write evolved; but that was not his own word, nor his theory of the origin of his ideas. He claimed that they came to him when he escaped his own control. I have forgotten many of the details and examples which he used to give in explanation of his doctrine, and should not remember them at all after so many years, save that at various times I have had similar experiences, and that I have been often reminded of them by the modern discussions of psychology, and especially of the operations of the subjective mind. He said that he was led into his view from thinking about his dreams which were beyond control of the will. His next step was to observe that he sometimes dreamed when awake; that is, thoughts came into his mind without conscious effort, and at times when his head was wholly vacant or wholly occupied with his business. Many things were made clear to him in this manner, and he had come to the conclusion that the best way to get the wisdom enjoined by the Bible and learned men, was to escape from yourself, in short, to become passive. In long summer days, slowly travelling his circuit of some forty miles, calling at every house where he was well known, and must needs be in no haste to trade, (for country people were never sure of what they wanted until they looked the cart over), he had plenty of time to resign himself to the involuntary and dreamlike states of mind, which solved for him the questions in which he was most interested. I was not so much impressed that such notions should come from a tin pedler as by the notions themselves; for at that period the democracy of our New England towns considered and treated a pedler as a man and a brother. His business was not regarded as demeaning, and frequently was an apprenticeship to that of a store keeper, and he might, and sometimes did, become the rich merchant of a great city. Many young men peddled small wares, books and pictures between terms to help themselves in paying for their education. So Reuben Daboll was no phenomenon; but his philosophy was phenomenal, at least to me, and kept me awake on the nights when the evening had been spent with him. It kept me awake, I say, for I never could reason far, and trying to think gave me a headache. I was perplexed by a thousand problems, my own, and those propounded by my companions and elders, and others suggested in books; and I wondered if Daboll's way was not an easier and shorter method of answer than the pros and cons of argument. It is interesting now for me to reflect upon the two influences following each other so closely, that were quickening my own faculties; for they were in direct contrast with each other; one, the animated debates and attempted logical presentation of a subject with its related facts, as presented at the Worcester Academy; and this new method of passive receptivity, this opening of the inner eye of the mind to receive impressions. It was a long time before I could experiment with any success in this new direction, for I was of an active and impatient temperament, longing to hurry to an end that I might begin something new, and wishing to arrive rather than to profit by each day's march. As I grew to maturity, the latter method was more congenial and became of more practical use to me, and one of my favorite mottoes has been, "Our thoughts are a pious reception."

The winter school being over in the spring, I returned to Worcester Academy feeling older and more sobered. I began Latin with a dim idea of going to college, how and when, I did not dare to forecast. I was not as happy as formerly in the school. The debates, compositions and declamations interested me less, and I should have been quite dull except for some young girls at the Oread Institute. This institution had just been opened on the hill, directly opposite our academy. It was not within speaking distance, but was within writing and signalling distance. All intercourse between the girl students and ourselves was prohibited. I have frequently noticed this juxtaposition of schools for the sexes, and also that laws of non-intercourse are enacted for no other purpose than to make their infringement the more tempting and delightful. My chum knew one of the Oreads, a girl from his own village; with this key we carried the citadel. We established a post office in the neighboring stone wall and arranged many a clandestine meeting, walk or drive. The girl whom I had chosen for my devotions was from the White Mountains of New Hampshire. She wore her hair in long curls, that fell over her neck and shoulders, and were constantly straggling over her face. Then with a toss of her comely head and a pretty gesture of her hand she would throw them back. This little trick captivated me and fixed my fate. She constantly came between me and the Latin declensions and conjugations that I was trying to memorize. However, I was saved from anything like a formal attachment by her early announcement to me that she was engaged to the son of an ex-governor of New Hampshire. I had reason to suspect afterward that this was a subterfuge to forestall any serious consequences from our intercourse. If so, she was a wise maiden, and whatever claims we men may arrogate to ourselves, women are better tacticians than we in their personal relations. With this barrier, thus timely erected, I was kept on my good behavior and we amused ourselves with each other's company in many a stolen woodland walk, and in a frequent defrauding of the Worcester post-office of its revenues. She wrote a tiny hand and could crowd more upon a page than I could upon four. I treasured her notes in my inmost pocket, and our secret correspondence gave me almost as deep a joy as did our companionship.

It was at this time I began to make verses, as much from an imitative instinct as from my sentimental relation with the pretty Oread; for there was now in the school a young man who set up for a poet and was much admired by us all. It seems to me he must have had a sense of musical rhythm, for there has remained in my ear ever since a stanza of his which I caught as he read it to a little coterie of students. There is nothing in it save its melody.

> "The while amid the greenwood
> Whistled the summer breeze
> Fair Mantua's maiden swore to wed
> Her loving Genoese."

Those two names, Mantua and Genoese, had a wonderful, faraway imaginative association for me, and still have. Matthew Arnold's magic of poetry, magical words and lines, explain all its charm for me. A feeling beyond the words or the sense is what I require in poetry. In vain did I try to express in rhyme what I felt. The lines halted for the last word. I never ventured to read them to my Oread or fellow students. Thus I cherished two secrets and discovered that the private indulgence of verse-making is almost as sweet as a hidden love. The terms of the Academy and the Oread Institute ended on the same day, and I parted from my sweetheart never to meet again.

FARM HAND

What to do with myself during the long summer vacation was the next question. My money was fast wasting in spite of my economies. There were no country schools open to male teachers in summer. My sister advised me to find employment on a farm. I thought at once of Bellingham, and my dear Uncle Lyman. He did not want help and eventually I hired myself to another uncle who lived in the extreme southern part of the town, close upon the boundary of Rhode Island. My wages were to be twelve dollars per month with board. My uncle's wife was my father's only surviving sister. Their children were married and settled elsewhere. All that was left to them was a large farm and old age. The one made them rather poorer than richer; the other brought upon them a growing habit of penuriousness, gloom and irritability. I was expected to do all the heavy work and most of the chores, except the milking; that, they would allow no one to do, for fear of not squeezing out the last drop. My aunt still made butter and cheese to sell, and in this work I usually helped her the first thing in the morning before the regular day's work. We had breakfast at sunrise, often before. After breakfast my uncle went into the sitting-room where:

> "He waled a portion with judicious care,
> 'And let us worship God,' he says, with solemn air."

I suppose that is what he did, for I could hear the low mumble of his voice and occasionally catch a scriptural phrase, but neither my aunt nor myself participated in this mockery of family prayers. She said she had too much to do, and she could not spare me from the cheese tub and the churn. She scolded her husband for his contributions to the church, and begrudged every cent that was spent. She had Franklin's prudential maxims at her tongue's end, besides many another gathered in the course of her long life of thrift and hard work. She never rested from her labors until the Sabbath. Our food was of the coarsest kind, but well cooked, and work and hunger were sauce enough. She baked once a week in a great brick oven; her other daily cooking was done by an open fire. Brown bread and cheese were the staff of our life, and I became more fond of them than of any viands I have since eaten. In vain have I besought my household to discover the recipe of my aunt's brown loaves. Who can recover for me the relish that went with them? With this aged couple I led a lonely yet healthful life. I came nearer to the earth than ever before; I mean her dirt, her stones, her odors and dews as well as to cows, sheep and horses, whose closer relation to the soil insensibly affects those who have the care of them. I felt myself a brother to the ox that I yoked and guided along the furrow. My nigh ox came from the pasture at my call and would lick my hand and stretch out his neck to be stroked. The whole barnyard was friendly, and I took pleasure, having none other, in the signs of it. The neighbors were few and I saw nothing of them. One young man sometimes called, but as his interest in me appeared to consist in a desire to save my soul his visits distressed me. It was my singular fortune through my childhood and early youth, to have been followed by soul savers. At last in desperation I told him that I was not sure as yet that I had a soul to save; when I had, I would consider his propositions. Whereupon he went his way and reported that I was a Universalist, that being in Bellingham the most opprobrious of names, in consequence of an ancient feud between the Baptist and Universalist churches. The Baptists had come off conquerers; the name, however, remained; and an indefinable name of reproach is a convenient thing to have in a country neighborhood.

I have mentioned the penuriousness of my employers. In the

case of my uncle it was exhibited in the most extraordinary, amusing, yet harmless ways. He never could pass by an old, bent, used-up nail, bit of string, pin or a straight stick without picking it up and putting it away. The collar of his coat and front of his gaudy flannel vest were stuck full of pointless pins and eyeless needles. The shed opposite the house was a museum of rubbish, odds and ends of the most worthless articles neatly sorted, tied up in small bundles and hung about the sides of the building. It was a well-developed mania with him, having acquired it through his long years of money getting and saving, and in larger matters, which had made him a well-to-do farmer. Although now old, he was a well-preserved man; there was still a wholesome red spot in his cheek, and a gleam of youth in his eye. His movements were so deliberate and slow that it was impossible that he could ever have worn himself out with work. He would pause between every hill that he hoed and make some remark, or look up at the sun for the time of the day. He could not mow a straight swath because he was always nicking in and out for some straw left by other mowers. When he harnessed his aged horse, as reliable as an ox to drive, and not much faster, he would go over and over every buckle and strap to make sure that all was safe, in the meantime talking to him in a soothing voice as if he expected every moment that he would run away. If Jim had a strong point it was in standing still. When he sneezed he used to say, "I guess I am good for another day," and like his wife he had a ready proverb for everything. Seldom could I catch the whole of it, for he sputtered in his speech and had a falsetto voice. It was evident that he had acquired his property by exceeding thrift, rather than labor, by that ancient all-pervading custom of the New England farmer of doing without and making things last another year.

I had promised myself to do some studying during the summer, but found that the long hours of labor and fatigue at their end unfitted me for anything save rest and sleep. I scarcely opened a book of any kind. I had a volume of Macauly's Essays with me in which I read a little on the Sabbath. On rainy days I stole away to the hay mow and read one of Jane Porter's novels which I found in the house. I attempted to commit to memory the whole of the Lady of the Lake, but got no farther than the first canto, and the songs interspersed through the others. These songs I recited in the field, and they were a great comfort to me. Little do the poets know in what strange, obscure places, and in what lonely, unknown hearts their verses find lodgment. It is not necessary that one should contend that Scott is the greatest of poets, who thought so for a single summer.

With thirty dollars in my purse and a blue camlet suit made of a cloak, which had been my father's best outer garment, I returned to Worcester Academy. I made a resolution, which I kept, to have no more intimacies with the Oreads, and to devote myself to study. I still cherished the idea of college, although it seemed as distant as ever. I began to be interested in public affairs and attended the first convention of the Free Soil party which was held in Worcester. I heard Charles Sumner and Charles Allen speak. Sumner appealed to my sympathies, Allen to my reason. Allen argued, Sumner was eloquent. Most young men in New England had hitherto been admirers of Webster and Clay, and termed themselves Whigs. The truth was they were called to whatever was eloquence. They worshipped the greatness of sounding, patriotic periods. How we admired Kossuth, and immediately paid him the shallow compliment of wearing a Kossuth hat. I also thought I was a Whig, much to the sorrow of my mother, whose sympathies were with the Abolitionists. After the Free Soil convention I was a Free Soiler, and such I continued, casting my first vote for John C. Fremont. At this time Worcester was the favorite place for every kind of convention of the friends of progress. Anti-slavery, Non-resistance and Women's Rights. I heard all the strange and strong speakers and advocates on those free and lively platforms. I heard Garrison, Phillips, May, Quincy, Pillsbury, the Fosters, Sojourner Truth, Burleigh, Lucretia Mott, and Ernestine Rose. The last speaker, a handsome, modishly dressed New York Jewess, converted me to the cause of woman. In a short time I was an enthusiastic reformer all along the line. Probably there has been no period in our history so charged with new and revolutionary ideas as that from 1835 to 1850. It was a good time to be alive and to be near the center of agitation in Massachusetts. I heard both church and state and the whole structure of society attacked. Whatever other reform might be under discussion these were sure to receive the hardest blows; strike, and spare not, was the watchword. For me the great event in my personal experience and awakening at this period, was not especially connected with the reforms that I have named. One small book very much in common with my former limited reading and enthusiasms for celebrated men, shook me to the center of my being. It was Emerson's Representative Men, recently published. Carelessly looking over the volumes on Mr. Grout's counter in Worcester, I took it up, attracted by its title, for I was always hungering for stories of eminent men, always hoping to find the secret of their greatness, that I might use it for my own advancement. I stood and read a few pages, laid down the book, but felt that I must read it through. After some battling between my purse and desire, desire won, and I bought the precious volume at the cost of my breakfast for several weeks, so slender were my resources. In the course of three or four years I added to my library Milton's poems, a volume of Tennyson and three of Potter's translation of Euripides; the latter, not because I wanted it, but because I happened to have made the final bid at a book auction. In Representative Men I found the meat my nature craved. In all previous histories and biographies that I had read, there was much going round and about poets and heroes, an external, academic treatment; with Emerson I seemed to come nearer the possible ideal which was already vaguely outlined in my mind. Besides there was much else than Napoleon and Shakespeare in the pages. There were the moral and poetic insights, and, moreover, there was the style, the vital and penetrating Emersonianism, which aroused, and no doubt, dazzled the youthful and impressionable reader. Emerson's terse epigrammatic method of writing was congenial to my inability to follow difficult logic. His style seemed to me the poetical foil of all the prosers of all time. Through the reading of this book eventually I became acquainted with Emerson,

Alcott and Thoreau. They became my teachers; I followed them until, by their guidance, I was enlarged enough to find my own way into companionship with those poets and thinkers, who have endured through the ages. May I never forget to acknowledge my debt to those men of Concord, my earliest masters in fidelity to ideals and the inward light.

CONCLUSION

I began to write these confidences of boyhood for my own pleasure. If I were to continue them into manhood I could not find nor distinguish myself. It would be like emerging suddenly from solitude into a crowd. The bright days of childhood easily separate themselves from all later time, and are painted with the free pencil of the imagination. I have now come almost to the wide gateways of the world where I must join the indistinguishable procession and begin to forget myself in its alluring enchantments.

With the discovery of certain books of ancient history, Plutarch, Euripides and Emerson's Essays there came an unexpected close to my student life at the Worcester Academy. Several of my classmates and myself agreed that we could be better fitted for college at Phillips Academy, Andover, than where we were, and accordingly we put ourselves under the tuition of Dr. Samuel H. Taylor, at that time the most eminent school and drill-master in New England. Under him I just escaped becoming a classical scholar and also nearly lost the chance of ever acquiring a love for the classics; for it was drill, paradigms, rules, exceptions, scansion, in short, all that pertains to the external apparatus of the Greek and Latin tongues. Often we spent two hours on eight lines of Homer. The father of literature became a Procrustean, grammatical bed on which we were to be stretched, and it did nearly exterminate every one of us. For my own part, I was possessed with an intemperate haste to read Homer straight through as fast as I could; for I felt, without exactly knowing, that there was something in the epic I wanted, yes, I needed and must have. Checked in this by the rigors of the recitation room I lost much of my interest in study, and spent the time which was supposed to be given to text books in reading all the classic and English poetry I could find, and in valorous attempts at composition, both prose and verse. This I by no means now regret, and rejoice that my tuition escaped the Spartan discipline no less than the present pragmatical curricula.

At length I was fitted for college and admitted to Harvard. Misfortunes culminated at the same moment. I did not remain. I was too ill for study, and suddenly the bottom of my perfidious purse dropped out. Bitter was my disappointment. But in another year I began a new career which brought me happiness, new opportunities, new friends and dividends from Utopian investments. Health and hope, my natural inheritance, returned. Boyhood was gone, but not the invincible boy.

As in the Parable I had traveled far, uncertain of the road. My diet had been mostly husks, but how sweet! Arriving at last at hospitable doors, I could receive without penitence, without tears the welcome long prepared for me. Thenceforth I submitted myself with more patience and trust to the destiny which had been awaiting me throughout my apprenticeships. My destiny became my choice.

AVE ATGUE VALE

I shall not pass this way again;
But near by is the town where I was born;
   I loved it well.

And near my heart my mother State;
She wreathed her sword with freedom, learning, law
   When tyrants fell.

Three words from Athens held me long;
Nothing-too-much, proportion, harmony;
   By these excel.

I never hurried for the goal,
But like the tortoise travelled steadily,
   Sans band, sans bell.

Born when the star of Spring arose,
Haply my auspices were cast for calm
   Of wood and dell.

Form I admired and sounds and scents;
Motion of waters, silences of stars—
   Mighty their spell!

No senate called me from the plow;
No hundred thousand readers read my books—
   They did not sell.

Many the friends when life was new
Heaven sent to me, but now, alas, reclaimed;
   Sound, Muse, their knell.

You, who hereafter pass this way,
Remember him who made this simple book
   And say farewell.

Choose from Thousands of 1stWorldLibrary Classics By

A. M. Barnard	Booth Tarkington	Edward Everett Hale
Ada Leverson	Boyd Cable	Edward J. O'Biren
Adolphus William Ward	Bram Stoker	Edward S. Ellis
Aesop	C. Collodi	Edwin L. Arnold
Agatha Christie	C. E. Orr	Eleanor Atkins
Alexander Aaronsohn	C. M. Ingleby	Eleanor Hallowell Abbott
Alexander Kielland	Carolyn Wells	Eliot Gregory
Alexandre Dumas	Catherine Parr Traill	Elizabeth Gaskell
Alfred Gatty	Charles A. Eastman	Elizabeth McCracken
Alfred Ollivant	Charles Amory Beach	Elizabeth Von Arnim
Alice Duer Miller	Charles Dickens	Ellem Key
Alice Turner Curtis	Charles Dudley Warner	Emerson Hough
Alice Dunbar	Charles Farrar Browne	Emilie F. Carlen
Allen Chapman	Charles Ives	Emily Bronte
Alleyne Ireland	Charles Kingsley	Emily Dickinson
Ambrose Bierce	Charles Klein	Enid Bagnold
Amelia E. Barr	Charles Hanson Towne	Enilor Macartney Lane
Amory H. Bradford	Charles Lathrop Pack	Erasmus W. Jones
Andrew Lang	Charles Romyn Dake	Ernie Howard Pie
Andrew McFarland Davis	Charles Whibley	Ethel May Dell
Andy Adams	Charles Willing Beale	Ethel Turner
Angela Brazil	Charlotte M. Braeme	Ethel Watts Mumford
Anna Alice Chapin	Charlotte M. Yonge	Eugene Sue
Anna Sewell	Charlotte Perkins Stetson	Eugenie Foa
Annie Besant	Clair W. Hayes	Eugene Wood
Annie Hamilton Donnell	Clarence Day Jr.	Eustace Hale Ball
Annie Payson Call	Clarence E. Mulford	Evelyn Everett-green
Annie Roe Carr	Clemence Housman	Everard Cotes
Annonaymous	Confucius	F. H. Cheley
Anton Chekhov	Coningsby Dawson	F. J. Cross
Archibald Lee Fletcher	Cornelis DeWitt Wilcox	F. Marion Crawford
Arnold Bennett	Cyril Burleigh	Fannie E. Newberry
Arthur C. Benson	D. H. Lawrence	Federick Austin Ogg
Arthur Conan Doyle	Daniel Defoe	Ferdinand Ossendowski
Arthur M. Winfield	David Garnett	Fergus Hume
Arthur Ransome	Dinah Craik	Florence A. Kilpatrick
Arthur Schnitzler	Don Carlos Janes	Fremont B. Deering
Arthur Train	Donald Keyhoe	Francis Bacon
Atticus	Dorothy Kilner	Francis Darwin
B.H. Baden-Powell	Dougan Clark	Frances Hodgson Burnett
B. M. Bower	Douglas Fairbanks	Frances Parkinson Keyes
B. C. Chatterjee	E. Nesbit	Frank Gee Patchin
Baroness Emmuska Orczy	E. P. Roe	Frank Harris
Baroness Orczy	E. Phillips Oppenheim	Frank Jewett Mather
Basil King	E. S. Brooks	Frank L. Packard
Bayard Taylor	Earl Barnes	Frank V. Webster
Ben Macomber	Edgar Rice Burroughs	Frederic Stewart Isham
Bertha Muzzy Bower	Edith Van Dyne	Frederick Trevor Hill
Bjornstjerne Bjornson	Edith Wharton	Frederick Winslow Taylor

Friedrich Kerst	Hayden Carruth	James Branch Cabell
Friedrich Nietzsche	Helent Hunt Jackson	James DeMille
Fyodor Dostoyevsky	Helen Nicolay	James Joyce
G.A. Henty	Hendrik Conscience	James Lane Allen
G.K. Chesterton	Hendy David Thoreau	James Lane Allen
Gabrielle E. Jackson	Henri Barbusse	James Oliver Curwood
Garrett P. Serviss	Henrik Ibsen	James Oppenheim
Gaston Leroux	Henry Adams	James Otis
George A. Warren	Henry Ford	James R. Driscoll
George Ade	Henry Frost	Jane Abbott
Geroge Bernard Shaw	Henry James	Jane Austen
George Cary Eggleston	Henry Jones Ford	Jane L. Stewart
George Durston	Henry Seton Merriman	Janet Aldridge
George Ebers	Henry W Longfellow	Jens Peter Jacobsen
George Eliot	Herbert A. Giles	Jerome K. Jerome
George Gissing	Herbert Carter	Jessie Graham Flower
George MacDonald	Herbert N. Casson	John Buchan
George Meredith	Herman Hesse	John Burroughs
George Orwell	Hildegard G. Frey	John Cournos
George Sylvester Viereck	Homer	John F. Kennedy
George Tucker	Honore De Balzac	John Gay
George W. Cable	Horace B. Day	John Glasworthy
George Wharton James	Horace Walpole	John Habberton
Gertrude Atherton	Horatio Alger Jr.	John Joy Bell
Gordon Casserly	Howard Pyle	John Kendrick Bangs
Grace E. King	Howard R. Garis	John Milton
Grace Gallatin	Hugh Lofting	John Philip Sousa
Grace Greenwood	Hugh Walpole	John Taintor Foote
Grant Allen	Humphry Ward	Jonas Lauritz Idemil Lie
Guillermo A. Sherwell	Ian Maclaren	Jonathan Swift
Gulielma Zollinger	Inez Haynes Gillmore	Joseph A. Altsheler
Gustav Flaubert	Irving Bacheller	Joseph Carey
H. A. Cody	Isabel Cecilia Williams	Joseph Conrad
H. B. Irving	Isabel Hornibrook	Joseph E. Badger Jr
H.C. Bailey	Israel Abrahams	Joseph Hergesheimer
H. G. Wells	Ivan Turgenev	Joseph Jacobs
H. H. Munro	J.G.Austin	Jules Vernes
H. Irving Hancock	J. Henri Fabre	Julian Hawthrone
H. R. Naylor	J. M. Barrie	Julie A Lippmann
H. Rider Haggard	J. M. Walsh	Justin Huntly McCarthy
H. W. C. Davis	J. Macdonald Oxley	Kakuzo Okakura
Haldeman Julius	J. R. Miller	Karle Wilson Baker
Hall Caine	J. S. Fletcher	Kate Chopin
Hamilton Wright Mabie	J. S. Knowles	Kenneth Grahame
Hans Christian Andersen	J. Storer Clouston	Kenneth McGaffey
Harold Avery	J. W. Duffield	Kate Langley Bosher
Harold McGrath	Jack London	Kate Langley Bosher
Harriet Beecher Stowe	Jacob Abbott	Katherine Cecil Thurston
Harry Castlemon	James Allen	Katherine Stokes
Harry Coghill	James Andrews	L. A. Abbot
Harry Houidini	James Baldwin	L. T. Meade

L. Frank Baum
Latta Griswold
Laura Dent Crane
Laura Lee Hope
Laurence Housman
Lawrence Beasley
Leo Tolstoy
Leonid Andreyev
Lewis Carroll
Lewis Sperry Chafer
Lilian Bell
Lloyd Osbourne
Louis Hughes
Louis Joseph Vance
Louis Tracy
Louisa May Alcott
Lucy Fitch Perkins
Lucy Maud Montgomery
Luther Benson
Lydia Miller Middleton
Lyndon Orr
M. Corvus
M. H. Adams
Margaret E. Sangster
Margret Howth
Margaret Vandercook
Margaret W. Hungerford
Margret Penrose
Maria Edgeworth
Maria Thompson Daviess
Mariano Azuela
Marion Polk Angellotti
Mark Overton
Mark Twain
Mary Austin
Mary Catherine Crowley
Mary Cole
Mary Hastings Bradley
Mary Roberts Rinehart
Mary Rowlandson
M. Wollstonecraft Shelley
Maud Lindsay
Max Beerbohm
Myra Kelly
Nathaniel Hawthrone
Nicolo Machiavelli
O. F. Walton
Oscar Wilde
Owen Johnson
P.G. Wodehouse
Paul and Mabel Thorne

Paul G. Tomlinson
Paul Severing
Percy Brebner
Percy Keese Fitzhugh
Peter B. Kyne
Plato
Quincy Allen
R. Derby Holmes
R. L. Stevenson
R. S. Ball
Rabindranath Tagore
Rahul Alvares
Ralph Bonehill
Ralph Henry Barbour
Ralph Victor
Ralph Waldo Emmerson
Rene Descartes
Ray Cummings
Rex Beach
Rex E. Beach
Richard Harding Davis
Richard Jefferies
Richard Le Gallienne
Robert Barr
Robert Frost
Robert Gordon Anderson
Robert L. Drake
Robert Lansing
Robert Lynd
Robert Michael Ballantyne
Robert W. Chambers
Rosa Nouchette Carey
Rudyard Kipling
Saint Augustine
Samuel B. Allison
Samuel Hopkins Adams
Sarah Bernhardt
Sarah C. Hallowell
Selma Lagerlof
Sherwood Anderson
Sigmund Freud
Standish O'Grady
Stanley Weyman
Stella Benson
Stella M. Francis
Stephen Crane
Stewart Edward White
Stijn Streuvels
Swami Abhedananda
Swami Parmananda
T. S. Ackland

T. S. Arthur
The Princess Der Ling
Thomas A. Janvier
Thomas A Kempis
Thomas Anderton
Thomas Bailey Aldrich
Thomas Bulfinch
Thomas De Quincey
Thomas Dixon
Thomas H. Huxley
Thomas Hardy
Thomas More
Thornton W. Burgess
U. S. Grant
Upton Sinclair
Valentine Williams
Various Authors
Vaughan Kester
Victor Appleton
Victor G. Durham
Victoria Cross
Virginia Woolf
Wadsworth Camp
Walter Camp
Walter Scott
Washington Irving
Wilbur Lawton
Wilkie Collins
Willa Cather
Willard F. Baker
William Dean Howells
William le Queux
W. Makepeace Thackeray
William W. Walter
William Shakespeare
Winston Churchill
Yei Theodora Ozaki
Yogi Ramacharaka
Young E. Allison
Zane Grey

www.ingramcontent.com/pod-product-compliance
Lightning Source LLC
Chambersburg PA
CBHW020002050426
42450CB00005B/283